PHYSICIAN-ASSISTED SUICIDE

PHYSICIAN-ASSISTED SUICIDE

Other books in the At Issue series:

PHYSICIAN-ASSISTED SUICIDE

Gail N. Hawkins, *Book Editor*

Daniel Leone, *President*
Bonnie Szumski, *Publisher*
Scott Barbour, *Managing Editor*

GREENHAVEN PRESS
SAN DIEGO, CALIFORNIA

GALE GROUP
™
THOMSON LEARNING
Detroit • New York • San Diego • San Francisco
Boston • New Haven, Conn. • Waterville, Maine
London • Munich

Library of Congress Cataloging-in-Publication Data

Physician-assisted suicide / Gail N. Hawkins, book editor.
    p. cm. — (At issue)
    Includes bibliographical references and index.
    ISBN 0-7377-1055-1 (pbk. : alk. paper) —
ISBN 0-7377-1056-X (lib. : alk. paper)
    1. Assisted suicide—Moral and ethical aspects. 2. Medical ethics. I. Hawkins, Gail N. II. At issue (San Diego, Calif.)

R726 .P4922   2002
174'.24—dc21   2001054325

Copyright © 2002 by Greenhaven Press,
an imprint of The Gale Group
10911 Technology Place, San Diego, CA 92127

Printed in the U.S.A.

Every effort has been made to trace owners of copyrighted material.

Contents

Introduction

On June 26, 1997, the U.S. Supreme Court ruled that individuals do not have a fundamental, constitutional right to physician-assisted suicide. This ruling reversed two previous decisions by U.S. courts of appeals. In the first case, *Washington State vs. Glucksberg*, the Ninth Circuit court had determined that a Washington state law prohibiting individuals from aiding in suicides was unconstitutional. The court supported its decision by concluding that individuals have a constitutionally protected right under the Due Process Clause of the Fourteenth Amendment to control the timing and method of their death. In *New York vs. Quill*, in a ruling similar to the Ninth Circuit's decision, the Second Circuit court of appeals had declared unconstitutional a New York state law that prohibited assisting someone in committing suicide. The court justified its decision by arguing that the law violated the Equal Protection Clause of the Fourteenth Amendment. Both courts' decisions had, in effect, recognized a constitutional "right to die."

Although the Supreme Court overturned the decisions of the two courts of appeals, its ruling did not put an end to the debate over assisted suicide. As Justice Sandra Day O'Connor noted, the Court concluded that there "is no generalized right to commit suicide." However, the Court emphasized that its decision and the Constitution do not place absolute restrictions on state law, leaving open the possibility for states to create their own laws to establish such a right. In addition, the Court indicated that laws that prohibit physician-assisted suicide could still be challenged in specific cases in the future. According to legal experts who evaluated the decision, the Court recognized that physician-assisted suicide is a complicated issue and that each case has a unique set of circumstances that must be evaluated separately. In short, the Court shifted the responsibility for this issue to the states, and by doing so it indirectly ensured that the controversy and legal battles over physician-assisted suicide will continue.

What is physician-assisted suicide?

There are varying degrees to which a person can be involved in hastening the death of a terminally ill individual. It is important to understand the terms for and distinctions between these degrees. Euthanasia, a word that is often associated with physician-assisted suicide, is defined by the *Merriam-Webster Dictionary* as "the act or practice of killing for reasons of mercy." There are two types of euthanasia: passive and active. Passive euthanasia takes place when life-saving measures are withheld or withdrawn and the terminally ill person is allowed to die of natural causes. A son's electing to take his mother off life-support machines, which leads to her death, would be an example of passive euthanasia. Today, there is little controversy and debate over passive euthanasia. The constitutional right of a patient (or if the patient is incompetent, the patient's guardian) to refuse treatment was established in 1976 by the Supreme Court's decision in the case of Karen Ann Quinlan. In 1975, Quinlan fell into an irreversible coma after a drug overdose and was put on a life-support system. Her parents, who wished to bring an end to their family's suffering, met resistance after requesting that their daughter be removed from life support. They fought a legal battle all the way to the Supreme Court. The Court decided in favor of Quinlan's parents and granted them the right to remove their daughter from the system, establishing a legal precedent for passive euthanasia.

In active euthanasia, a person actually causes the death of a terminally ill individual. For example, a person who gives a dying friend a lethal injection to hasten death would be performing active euthanasia. Although active euthanasia is presently illegal, many medical professionals claim that it is practiced in secrecy on a regular basis. Active euthanasia is highly controversial: Its critics argue that patients are often not informed of what is being done to them or are coerced into agreeing to the act.

Assisted suicide takes place when a dying person who wishes to precipitate death requests help in carrying out the act. There is a distinction between assisted suicide and euthanasia. In euthanasia, the dying patients may or may not be aware of what is happening to them and may or may not have requested to die. In an assisted suicide, the terminally ill person wants to die and has specifically asked for help. Physician-assisted suicide occurs when the individual assisting in the suicide is a doctor rather than a friend or family member. Because doctors are the people most familiar with their patients' medical condition and have knowledge of and access to the necessary means to cause certain death, terminally ill patients who have made the decision to end their lives often turn to their physicians for advice and help. Studies indicate, however, that many physicians are unwilling to provide their assistance in suicide because it conflicts with their ethical beliefs or because it is illegal.

The controversy over legalization

Much of the controversy surrounding physician-assisted suicide focuses on the debate over whether the practice should be legalized. Oregon is the only state in which physician-assisted suicide is legal. In 1994, voters in that state approved a referendum called the Death with Dignity Act, which was enacted in 1997. This law allows doctors to prescribe lethal doses of medication to mentally competent, terminally ill patients to use to hasten their own deaths. Between 1998 and 2000, ninety-six lethal prescriptions were written, and seventy patients took the fatal doses. In the rest of the country, the practice remains illegal.

Supporters of legalization believe that terminally ill individuals have the right to end their own lives in some instances. Because physician-assisted suicide is illegal in most states, they maintain, many patients are unable to get the help necessary to end their lives and must involuntarily endure extreme pain and suffering. Others argue that physician-assisted suicide must be legalized for purposes of regulation. They contend that in spite of current law, the practice is conducted regularly in secrecy; therefore, the potential for abuse already exists. According to

Cheryl Smith, former staff attorney for the Hemlock Society, "Legalization, with medical record documentation and reporting requirements, will enable authorities to regulate the practice and guard against abuses, while punishing the real offenders."

On the other hand, opponents of physician-assisted suicide argue that widespread legalization would cause abuse rather than reduce or control it. They maintain that legalized assisted suicide would lead to the deaths of patients who do not really wish to die. For example, they contend that influential doctors or family members, unrestricted by law, may persuade patients to choose death or that greedy insurance companies may pressure doctors to control insurance costs by ending lives prematurely.

Others worry that universal legalization of assisted suicide would be the first step down the "slippery slope" that would lead to widespread, unregulated mercy killing of individuals whom society considers undesirable or whose lives have been arbitrarily deemed not worth living. As expressed by legal experts Robert George and William Porth, "It is not unrealistic to fear that government may assume what began as a private prerogative, and move from making life-and-death decisions for the comatose, to making them for the insane, for the retarded, for those of less than average intelligence, and finally for those who are entirely rational and intelligent, but whose desire to cling to life brands them as obstinate, uncooperative, and just plain unreasonable." These fears lead many to oppose physician-assisted suicide even under carefully regulated conditions.

The legalization of physician-assisted suicide is an extremely sensitive, complicated, and controversial topic. If future legislation is to be successful, it will need to protect both the rights of terminally ill patients who rationally choose death and the rights of weak or incompetent patients who do not wish to die. This anthology, *At Issue: Physician-Assisted Suicide*, explores a variety of perspectives on the legal, ethical, and moral aspects of physician-assisted suicide.

1

Physician-Assisted Suicide Is Sometimes Morally Justified

Dan W. Brock

Dan W. Brock is professor of philosophy and director of the Center for Biomedical Ethics in the School of Medicine at Brown University. He is the author of Life and Death: Philosophical Essays in Biomedical Ethics.

Physician-assisted suicide is morally justified when voluntarily chosen by a terminally ill patient whose life has become unendurable and whose judgment is not impaired by depression. Assisted suicide, when motivated by respect for the wishes of the patient, provides the terminally ill with a dignified, humane death.

There are two central and distinct moral issues about physician-assisted suicide.[1] First, is physician-assisted suicide morally justified in any individual cases? Second, would it be ethically justified for public and legal policy to permit physician-assisted suicide? This chapter is concerned only with the first of these questions, and I shall argue the affirmative answer. The affirmative case for a public policy permitting physician-assisted suicide is in my view more complex and less decisive, though nevertheless also sound. But my concern will be broader than the first question in one important respect. The argument that I shall make applies in nearly all essentials to voluntary active euthanasia as well as physician-assisted suicide, and I shall begin by indicating why I believe the two are not importantly different morally. (For brevity and unless explicitly indicated otherwise, I shall hereafter use "assisted suicide" to refer to physician-assisted suicide and "euthanasia" to refer to voluntary active euthanasia.)

In the recent bioethics literature some have endorsed assisted suicide but not euthanasia, even in individual cases and not only for public policy.[2] Moreover, the policy proposals that in the last few years have been brought to legislatures or to the public in state referenda in nearly all cases have applied only to assisted suicide and not to euthanasia. Are they sufficiently different that the moral arguments that apply to one often do not apply to the other? First, what is the difference between assisted suicide and euthanasia? A paradigm case of assisted suicide is a patient's end-

From "Physician-Assisted Suicide Is Sometimes Morally Justified," by Dan W. Brock in *Physician-Assisted Suicide*, edited by Robert F. Weir (Bloomington: Indiana University Press, 1997). Copyright © 1997 by Indiana University Press. Reprinted with permission.

ing his or her life with a lethal dose of a medication requested of and provided by a physician for that purpose. A paradigm case of euthanasia is a
physician's administering the lethal dose, often because the patient is unable to do so. The only difference that need exist between the two is the
person who actually administers the lethal dose—the physician or the patient. In each, the physician plays an active and necessary causal role in
providing the lethal dose. In each, the intent of the patient and physician
is to pursue a course of action that will end in the patient's death.

In assisted suicide the patient acts last (for example, Janet Adkins
pushed the button after Dr. Jack Kevorkian hooked her up to his suicide
machine), whereas in euthanasia the physician acts last by performing
the physical equivalent of pushing the button. In both cases, however,
the choice rests fully with the patient in the sense that neither will take
place without the patient's desire for them; of course, in each the physician must also be willing to play his or her role. In both the patient acts
last in the sense of retaining the right to change his or her mind until the
point at which the lethal process becomes irreversible. How could there
be a substantial moral difference between the two based only on this
small difference in the part played by the physician in the causal process
resulting in death? Of course, it might be held that the moral difference
is obvious and important—in euthanasia the physician kills the patient,
whereas in assisted suicide the patient kills him- or herself. But this is mis-
leading at best. In assisted suicide the physician and patient act together
to kill the patient. To see this, suppose a physician supplied a lethal dose
to a patient with the knowledge and intent that the patient will wrong-
fully administer it to another. We would have no difficulty in morality or
the law recognizing this as a case of joint action to bring about another's
death, or to kill, for which both are responsible. The physician is involved
in killing in both assisted suicide and euthanasia, and so we will have to
address the morality of killing later in this chapter.

---

*Some argue that because in assisted suicide the
patient must take the final physical act that results
in his or her death, there is greater certainty of the
patient's voluntary resolve to die than when the
physician performs that act.*

If there is no significant, intrinsic moral difference between assisted
suicide and euthanasia, it is also difficult to see why public or legal policy
should permit one but not the other; worries about abuse or about giving
anyone dominion over the lives of others seem also to apply equally to either. Some argue that because in assisted suicide the patient must take the
final physical act that results in his or her death, there is greater certainty
of the patient's voluntary resolve to die than when the physician performs
that act. In some cases this may be true, but there are also cases of euthanasia in which the voluntary resolve of the patient to die is not in significant doubt. However, I shall not pursue the policy issue here, but I shall
take the arguments developed below about individual cases of physician-
assisted suicide to apply both to assisted suicide and to euthanasia.

My concern here will be only with *voluntary* cases of assisted suicide or euthanasia, that is, with cases in which a clearly competent patient makes a fully voluntary and persistent request for assisted suicide or euthanasia. Perhaps the assumption of voluntariness is implicit in the very concept of physician-assisted suicide, either in the condition that the patient performs the final physical act of using the means to end his or her life or in the notion of the physician assisting the patient, but I have said that my argument applies to active euthanasia as well, and voluntariness is not implicit there. Involuntary euthanasia, in which a competent patient explicitly refuses or opposes receiving euthanasia, and nonvoluntary euthanasia, in which a patient is incompetent and unable to express his or her wishes about euthanasia, are both possible but will not be my concern here. Finally, I will be concerned with assisted suicide and euthanasia where the motive of those who perform them is to respect the wishes of the patient and to provide the patient with a "good death"; only in such cases is the physician's participation morally justified.

A last introductory point is that I will be examining only secular arguments about assisted suicide and euthanasia, though of course many people's attitudes to them are inextricable from their religious views. Even if an individual's religious and moral views on this question are deeply connected, the moral justification for his or her position cannot consist simply in an appeal to religious authority. If the individual claims to offer a moral position on the issue, I believe that position must be stated and defended with arguments that do not presuppose or appeal to the authority of a particular religion and its beliefs and principles. The content of the moral reason or argument offered in secular terms can be the same as the content of the reasons that particular religions offer for their tenets and positions, but it must be offered as persuasive in its own terms, not only from within the standpoint or authority of the particular religion. (I also take this secular focus to be appropriate for public policy in a pluralistic society like our own; public policy should not be based on religious views reasonably rejected by a substantial portion of the society, though, since public policy is not my concern here, I shall not pursue or defend this claim.) Even if the position I will defend here is correct that assisted suicide and euthanasia are sometimes morally justified, I will take that to mean only that they would be morally permissible and justified in those circumstances. This is compatible with a position that I would also support, that anyone who has serious religious objections to them need not ask for them for him- or herself nor take any part in them when asked to do so by others.

The ethical argument for assisted suicide and euthanasia

The central ethical argument for assisted suicide and euthanasia is familiar. It is that the very same two fundamental ethical values supporting the consensus of patients' rights to decide about life-sustaining treatment also support the ethical permissibility of assisted suicide and euthanasia in some circumstances. And this implies that acceptance of assisted suicide and euthanasia is not as radical a moral departure from the current consensus and practice giving patients the right to decide to forgo life support, as is commonly supposed. These values are individual self-determination or autonomy and individual well-being. By self-determination, as it bears on assisted suicide and euthanasia, I mean people's interest in making important decisions about their lives for themselves according to their own values or conceptions of a good life and in being left free to act on those decisions. Self-determination is valuable because it permits people to form and to live in accordance with their own conception of a good life, at least within the bounds of justice and consistent with not preventing others from doing so as well. In exercising self-determination people exercise significant control over their lives and thereby take responsibility for their lives and for the kinds of persons they become. A central aspect of human dignity and the moral worth of persons lies in individuals' capacity to direct their lives in this way. The value of exercising self-determination presupposes some minimum of decision-making capacities or competence, which thus limits the scope of assisted suicide or euthanasia supported by self-determination; it does not apply, for example, in cases of serious dementia or treatable clinical depression that impair the individual's decision-making capacity.

Physicians are moral and professional agents whose own self-determination or integrity should be respected as well.

Individual self-determination has special importance in choices about the time and manner of one's death, including assisted suicide and euthanasia. Most people are very concerned about the nature of the last stage of their lives. This reflects not just a fear of experiencing substantial pain or suffering or of being abandoned by loved ones when dying, but also a desire to retain dignity and control to the extent possible during this last period of life. Death is today increasingly preceded by a long period of significant physical and mental decline, due in part to the technological interventions of modern medicine designed to stave off death. Many people adjust to their disability and dependency and find meaning and value in new activities and ways. Others find the impairments and burdens in the last stage of their lives at some point sufficiently great to make life no longer worth living. For some patients near death, maintaining the quality of one's life, avoiding great pain or suffering, maintaining one's dignity, and ensuring that others remember us as we wish them to become of paramount importance and outweigh merely extending one's life. But there is no single, objectively correct answer for everyone regarding when, if at all, one's life when critically or terminally ill becomes, all things considered, a burden and unwanted. If self-determination is a fundamental value, then the great variability among people on this question makes it especially important that individuals control to the extent possible the manner, circumstances, and timing of their dying and death.

The other main value that supports assisted suicide and euthanasia is individual well-being. It might seem that protecting and promoting individual well-being must always conflict with a person's self-determination when the person requests assisted suicide or euthanasia, but it is important to understand why this is not so. Life itself is commonly understood to be a central good for persons, often valued for its own sake, as well as necessary for the pursuit of all other goods within a life. But when a competent patient decides to forgo all further life-sustaining treatment, then the patient, either explicitly or implicitly, commonly decides that the best life possible for him or her with treatment is of sufficiently poor quality that it is worse than no further life at all. Life is then no longer considered a benefit by the patient but has now become without value or meaning and a burden. The same judgment underlies a request for assisted suicide or euthanasia—continued life is then seen by the patient as no longer a benefit, but now a burden. Especially in the often severely compromised and debilitated states of many critically ill or dying patients, there is no objective standard but only the competent patient's judgment of whether continued life is no longer a benefit.

Of course, sometimes conditions such as clinical depression call into question whether the patient has made a competent choice, either to forego life-sustaining treatment or to seek assisted suicide or euthanasia, and then the patient's choice need not be evidence that continued life is no longer a benefit for him or her.[3] Just as with decisions about treatment, a determination of incompetence can warrant not honoring the patient's request for assisted suicide or euthanasia; in the case of treatment, we then transfer decisional authority to a surrogate, though in the case of assisted suicide or voluntary euthanasia a determination that the patient is incompetent to make that choice means that neither should take place.

The value or right of self-determination of patients does not entitle them to compel physicians to act contrary to physicians' own moral or professional values. Physicians are moral and professional agents whose own self-determination or integrity should be respected as well. If performing assisted suicide or euthanasia becomes legally permissible but conflicts with a particular physician's reasonable understanding of his or her moral or professional responsibilities, the care of a patient who requests assisted suicide or euthanasia should be transferred to another. But the ethical issue with which I am concerned here is the moral permissibility or justification of performing either assisted suicide or euthanasia by those who do not have moral or professional objections to it.

Typical cases of stopping life-sustaining treatment are killing, not allowing to die, although they are cases of ethically justified killing.

Most opponents of assisted suicide and euthanasia do not deny that there are some cases in which the values of patient self-determination and well-being support them. Instead, opponents commonly offer two kinds of arguments against assisted suicide and euthanasia which they take to outweigh or override this support. The first kind of argument is my concern here—that in any individual case where considerations of the patient's self-determination and well-being do support assisted suicide or euthanasia, they are nevertheless always ethically wrong or impermissible. The second kind of argument is that even if in some individual cases assisted suicide or euthanasia may not be ethically wrong, it nonetheless would not be ethically sound or wise public and legal policy to permit them. While I do not pursue this second kind of argument here, it is important to distinguish it so that it is clear that the position I defend here, that assisted suicide and euthanasia are morally justified in some individual cases, is not determinative of whether public and legal policy should ever permit them.

Euthanasia is deliberate killing

In order to state the argument of the opponent of assisted suicide and euthanasia in its strongest form and to avoid unnecessary complexity in exposition, I shall focus in this section on euthanasia. The claim that any individual instance of euthanasia is a case of deliberate killing of an innocent person is, with only minor qualifications, correct. Unlike forgoing life-sustaining treatment, commonly understood as allowing to die, euthanasia is clearly killing, understood as depriving of life or causing the death of a living being. While providing morphine for pain relief at doses where the risk of respiratory depression and an earlier death may be a foreseen but unintended side effect of treating the patient's pain, in a case of euthanasia the patient's death is deliberate or intended even if in both the physician's ultimate end may be respecting the patient's wishes. If the deliberate killing of an innocent person is wrong, euthanasia would be nearly always impermissible.

In the context of medicine, the ethical prohibition against deliberately killing the innocent derives some of its plausibility from the belief that nothing in the currently accepted practice of medicine is deliberate killing. Thus, in commenting on the "It's Over Debbie"[4] case in which a resident deliberately gave a patient a lethal dose of morphine, four prominent physicians and bioethicists, led by Willard Gaylin, could entitle their paper "Doctors Must Not Kill."[5] The belief that doctors do not kill requires the corollary belief that forgoing life-sustaining treatment, whether by not starting or by stopping treatment, is allowing to die, not killing. Common though this view is, I shall argue that it is confused and mistaken. Typical cases of stopping life-sustaining treatment are killing, not allowing to die, although they are cases of ethically justified killing. But if so, that shows that an unqualified ethical prohibition of the deliberate killing of innocent persons is indefensible and must be revised.

Why is the common view mistaken that stopping life-sustaining treatment is allowing to die and not killing? Consider the case of a patient terminally ill with amytrophic lateral sclerosis disease (ALS, or Lou Gehrig's disease). She is completely respirator dependent with no hope of ever being weaned from the respirator. She is unquestionably competent but finds her condition intolerable and persistently requests to be removed from the respirator and allowed to die. Most people and physicians would likely agree that the patient's physician should respect the patient's wishes and remove her from the respirator, though this will certainly cause the patient's death. The common understanding is that the physician thereby allows the patient to die. But is that correct?

Suppose the patient has a greedy and hostile son who mistakenly believes both that his mother will never decide to stop her life-sustaining treatment and that even if she did her physician would not respect her wishes and remove her from the respirator. Afraid that his inheritance will be dissipated by a long and expensive hospitalization, he enters his mother's room while she is sedated, extubates her, and she dies. Shortly thereafter the medical staff discovers what he has done and confronts the son. He replies, "I didn't kill her, I merely allowed her to die. It was her ALS disease that caused her death." I think this would rightly be dismissed as transparent sophistry—the son went into his mother's room and deliberately killed her. But, of course, the son performed just the same physical actions, did just the same thing, with all the same consequences for the patient, that the physician would have done. If that is so, then doesn't the physician also kill the patient when he extubates her and stops the respirator?

Killing vs. allowing to die

I underline immediately that there are important ethical differences between what the physician and the greedy son do. First, the physician acts with the patient's consent, whereas the son does not. Second, the physician acts with a good motive—to respect the patient's wishes and self-determination—whereas the son acts with a bad motive—to protect his own inheritance. Third, the physician acts in a social role through which he is legally authorized to carry out the patient's decision to stop treatment, whereas the son has no such authorization. These and perhaps other ethically important differences show that what the physician did was morally justified, whereas what the son did was morally wrong. What they do *not* show, however, is that the son killed while the physician allowed to die. One can either kill or allow to die with or without consent, with a good or bad motive, within or outside a social role that legally authorizes one to do so.

The difference between killing and allowing to die that I have been implicitly appealing to here is roughly the difference between acts and omissions resulting in death.[6] Both the physician and the greedy son act in a manner intended to cause death, do cause death, and so both kill; neither allows to die. One reason this conclusion is resisted is that on a different understanding of the distinction between killing and allowing to die, what the physician does is allow to die. In this account, the mother's ALS is a lethal disease whose normal progression is being held back or blocked by the life-sustaining respirator treatment. Removing this artificial intervention is then viewed as standing aside and allowing the patient to die of her underlying disease. I have argued elsewhere that this alternative account is deeply problematic, in part because it seems to have the unacceptable implication that what the greedy son also does is to allow to die, not kill.[7] Here I want to note two other reasons why the conclusion that stopping life support is killing is resisted.

The first reason is that killing is often understood, especially within medicine, as unjustified or wrongful causing of death; in medicine it is thought to be done only accidentally or negligently. It is also increasingly widely accepted that a physician is ethically justified in stopping life support in a case like that of the ALS patient. But if both of these beliefs are correct, then what the physician does cannot be killing and so instead must be allowing to die. Killing patients is not, to put it flippantly, understood to be part of a physician's job description. What is mistaken in this line of reasoning is the assumption that all killings are *unjustified or wrongful* causings of death. Instead, some killings are ethically justified, including most instances of stopping life support.

Another reason for resisting the conclusion that stopping life support is often killing is that it is psychologically uncomfortable. Suppose the physician had stopped the ALS patient's respirator and had made the son's claim, "I didn't kill her, I merely allowed her to die. It was her ALS disease that caused her death." The clue to the psychological role here is how naturally the "merely" modifies "allowed her to die." The characterization as allowing to die is meant to shift felt responsibility away from the agent—the physician—and to the lethal disease process that the physician merely allowed to proceed to the patient's death. Other language common in death and dying contexts plays a similar role; "letting nature take its course" or "stopping prolonging the dying process" both seem to shift responsibility from the physician who stops life support to the fatal disease process. However psychologically helpful these conceptualizations may be in making the difficult responsibility of a physician's role in the patient's death bearable, they nevertheless are confusions. Both physicians and family members can instead be helped to understand that it is the patient's decision and consent to stopping treatment that limits their responsibility for the patient's death and which shifts that responsibility to the patient.

The difference between killing and allowing to die that I have been implicitly appealing to here is roughly the difference between acts and omissions resulting in death.

Many who accept this understanding of the difference between killing and allowing to die as the difference between acts and omissions resulting in death have gone on to argue that killing is not in itself morally different from allowing to die.[8] In this account, very roughly, one kills when one performs an action that causes the death of a person (e.g., we are in a boat, you cannot swim, I push you overboard, and you drown), and one allows to die when one has the ability and opportunity to prevent the death of another, knows this, and omits doing so, with the result that the person dies (e.g., we are in a boat, you cannot swim, you fall overboard, I don't throw you an available life ring, and you drown). Those who see no moral difference between killing and allowing to die typically employ the strategy of comparing cases that differ in these and no other potentially morally important respects. This will allow people to consider whether the mere difference that one is a case of killing and the other of allowing to die matters morally, or whether instead it is other features that make most killings worse than most instances of allowing to die. Here is such a pair of cases.

> *Case 1.* A very gravely ill patient is brought to a hospital emergency room and sent up to the ICU. The patient begins

to develop respiratory failure that is likely to require intubation very soon. At that point the patient's family members and long-time physician arrive at the ICU and inform the ICU staff that there had been extensive discussion about future care with the patient when he was unquestionably competent. Given his grave and terminal illness as well as his state of debilitation, the patient had firmly rejected being placed on a respirator under any circumstances, and the family and physician produce the patient's advance directive to that effect. The ICU staff do not intubate the patient, who dies of respiratory failure.

Case 2. The same as Case 1 except that the family and physician are slightly delayed in traffic and arrive shortly after the patient has been intubated and placed on the respirator. The ICU staff extubate the patient, who dies of respiratory failure.

In Case 1 the patient is allowed to die, in Case 2 he is killed, but it is hard to see why what is done in Case 2 is significantly different morally than what is done in Case 1. It must be other factors that make most killings worse than most allowings to die, and if so, assisted suicide and euthanasia cannot be wrong simply because they are killing instead of allowing to die.

A rights approach to the morality of killing

Suppose that both my arguments are mistaken. Suppose that killing is worse than allowing to die and that withdrawing life support is not killing, although assisted suicide and euthanasia are. Assisted suicide and euthanasia still need not for that reason be morally wrong. To see this, we need to determine the basic principle for the moral evaluation of killing persons. What is it that makes paradigm cases of wrongful killing wrongful? One very plausible answer is that killing denies the victim a very great good over whose possession he or she should have control—continued life or a future. Our continued life or future is typically the object of one of our strongest desires. It can be thought of as a dispositional or standing desire, which typically becomes an occurrent desire, occupying an important place in one's conscious desires and plans, when one's life is threatened. Moreover, continued life is a necessary condition for being able to pursue and achieve any of one's other plans and purposes; loss of life brings the frustration of all of these plans and purposes as well. In a nutshell, wrongful killing typically deprives a person of a great and valued good—his or her future and all that the person wanted and planned to do in that future. It is important to see that there is another distinct moral idea at work in this account of the wrongness of killing besides that killing typically deprives the victim of a very great good, on which nearly all other goods for that person depend. The other idea is that one's life is a good over which, at least within limits, a person him- or herself should retain control.

Sometimes these two moral ideas or values can be in conflict, as, for example, when an apparently competent patient makes an informed and voluntary choice to refuse life-sustaining treatment that would restore the patient to full function and a life that most people would consider a life well worth having. Here the patient is exercising his or her right of control over his or her life and what is done to his or her body to give up the apparently very great good of continued life. If we cannot come to understand why the patient reasonably does not value that continued life or cannot find serious impairments in the patient's decision making or cannot persuade the patient to accept the treatment, then we may be forced to decide which value is more important, preserving the good of the patient's life or respecting the patient's right of control over his or her own life, that is, his or her self-determination or autonomy.

Public policy, as expressed in the law, gives competent patients the right to refuse any treatment, including life-sustaining treatment, and thereby gives greater weight to respecting the patient's right of control or self-determination regarding his or her own life. The law's resolution of this conflict in favor of self-determination recognizes not only the deep place of that value in our moral, cultural, and legal traditions but also the circumstance that when a competent individual rejects life-sustaining treatment he or she either no longer finds continued life a good or finds the means of gaining it unacceptable (for example, when Jehovah's Witness patients reject life-sustaining blood products). Our moral and cultural traditions, however, do not speak with one voice about how these values should be weighed when they are in conflict. Reasonable people can and do disagree about how this conflict should be resolved when an apparently worthwhile life is being given up by a competent patient.

Killing patients is not, to put it flippantly, understood to be part of a physician's job description.

In a comparable case in which a person with an apparently worthwhile life sought assisted suicide or euthanasia, most physicians and most persons probably would refuse to take part. But that is not at all the typical case in which assisted suicide or euthanasia is sought; nor is it the kind of case in which I am arguing that they are morally permissible and justified. Instead, in the typical and relevant case others view the competent individual's decision as quite reasonable, that continued life is no longer a good because that life is so filled with suffering and bereft of possibilities for the activities and experiences that make life valuable and meaningful. In such cases, the morally great good of continued life and the respect owed the patient's self-determination are not in conflict because continued life is no longer a great good but is now reasonably judged by the patient to be a burden and without value. Some physicians who give great weight to patient self-determination might be willing to participate in assisted suicide even when they cannot accept the patient's judgment that his or her life is no longer worth living. But many others would be willing to participate in assisted suicide or euthanasia only if they either share or at least view as reasonable the patient's judgment that his or her life is no longer worth living. In such cases, no significant good for the patient need be sacrificed in order to respect the patient's self-determination.

A natural expression of my account of the wrongness of killing is that people have a moral right not to be killed.[9] But the right not to be killed, like other rights, should he understood as waivable when the person makes a competent decision that continued life is no longer wanted or a good but is instead worse than no further life at all, and so wishes to die. In this rights view of the wrongness of killing, assisted suicide and euthanasia are properly understood as cases in which the person killed has waived his or her right not to be killed, thereby making the physician's action not a violation of that right.

This rights view of the wrongness of killing is not, of course, universally shared. Many people's moral views about killing have their origins in religious beliefs that human life comes from God and cannot be justifiably destroyed or taken away, either by the person whose life it is or by another. I noted earlier that I would be addressing only secular moral arguments regarding assisted suicide and euthanasia, and so will only reiterate two points made there. First, in a pluralistic society like our own with a strong commitment to freedom of religion, public policy should not be grounded in religious beliefs which many in that society reject. Second, if the position about the wrongness of killing rests on theological premises that many persons can and do reasonably reject, then those persons will have been given no reason why they should regard such killing as wrong.

The rejection of the rights view of the wrongness of killing, however, does not always have a religious basis. Some people believe it is always morally wrong deliberately to take an innocent human life—what is sometimes called a duty-based view on taking human life. The "innocence condition" may permit killing in self-defense or even in capital punishment under some interpretations, but not when a person seeks assisted suicide or euthanasia. If this moral prohibition does not derive from God, however, it is difficult to see what its moral basis can be. That basis can be neither that life is a very great good that should never be destroyed nor that one individual should never claim dominion over the life of another. As we have seen, sometimes the killing of an innocent person, in particular assisted suicide and euthanasia, does not conflict with but is instead supported by these two values. These are the moral values that support the rights account, not the duty account, of the morality of killing.

Good consequences

I have largely addressed the question of whether assisted suicide and euthanasia are in some cases morally permissible. I have argued that it is most importantly the patient's moral right to self-determination, together with the waiving of his or her right not to be killed, that grounds that moral permissibility. However, the moral case in support of assisted suicide and euthanasia is in some instances considerably stronger than "mere permissibility"; they are then not just permissible but justified. On most accounts of "moral permissibility," an action may be morally permissible even if it would be better if an agent did not do it or if doing it would be wrong.[10] But assisted suicide and euthanasia are not merely permissible in this sense; they are in some cases morally justified with strong moral reasons in support of them. We can see this best if we ask what other good consequences assisted suicide or euthanasia could produce besides the obvious one of granting to patients who seek them what they want.

Perhaps the most important good consequence of physician-assisted suicide or voluntary active euthanasia concerns patients whose lives while they are dying are filled with severe and unrelievable pain or suffering. When there is a life-sustaining treatment which, if forgone, will lead relatively quickly to death, then doing so can bring an end to these patients' suffering without recourse to assisted suicide or euthanasia. For patients with no life-sustaining treatment that can be withheld or withdrawn, however, assisted suicide or euthanasia may be the only release from their otherwise prolonged suffering and agony. This argument from mercy has always been the strongest argument for assisted suicide or euthanasia in those cases to which it applies.[11]

Some killings are ethically justified, including most instances of stopping life support.

The moral importance of relieving great pain and suffering is less controversial than is the frequency with which patients are forced to undergo untreatable agony that only assisted suicide or euthanasia could relieve. If we focus first on suffering caused by physical pain, it is crucial to distinguish pain that *could* be adequately relieved with modern methods of pain control, though it in fact is not, from pain that is relievable only by death.[12] For a variety of reasons, including some physicians' discomfort with prescribing large amounts of narcotics for fear of hastening the patient's death, as well as the lack of a publicly accessible means for assessing the amount of the patient's pain, many patients suffer pain that could be but is not relieved.

Specialists in controlling certain types of pain, for example the pain of terminally ill cancer patients, argue that there are very few patients whose pain could not be adequately controlled, though sometimes at the cost of so sedating them that they are effectively unable to interact with other people or their environment. Thus the argument from mercy in cases of physical pain can probably be met in the great majority of cases by providing adequate measures of pain relief. This should be a high priority, whatever one's view about assisted suicide or euthanasia—the relief of pain and suffering has long been, quite properly, one of the central goals of medicine.

Dying patients often undergo substantial psychological suffering, however, that is not fully or even principally the result of physical pain.[13] The knowledge about how to relieve this suffering is much more limited than in the case of relieving pain, and efforts to do so are probably more often unsuccessful. If the argument from mercy is extended, as it properly can be, to patients experiencing great and unrelievable psychological suffering, the numbers of patients to which it applies is much greater. In these cases, assisted suicide or euthanasia may be the only release from the patient's suffering.

A second good consequence of some instances of assisted suicide or euthanasia is that once death has been accepted, it is often more humane to end life quickly and peacefully, as can be done by assisted suicide or euthanasia, when that is what the patient wants. Such a death will often be seen as better than a more prolonged one in which the patient may be robbed of his or her dignity. People who suffer a sudden and unexpected death by dying quickly or in their sleep from a heart attack or stroke, for example, are often considered lucky to have died in this way instead of by a more drawn-out process. We care about how we die in part because we care about how others remember us, and we hope they will remember us as we were in "good times" with them and not as we might be when disease has robbed us of our dignity as human beings. As with much in the treatment and care of the dying, people's concerns differ in this respect, but for at least some people, assisted suicide or euthanasia will be a more humane death than what they have often experienced with other loved ones and might otherwise expect for themselves.

This aim of providing a patient with a better death is relevant to the objection to assisted suicide or euthanasia, that they are never necessary because it is always possible to withdraw or withhold nutrition and hydration from a patient, which will result in the patient's death without recourse to the active and more controversial interventions of assisted suicide or euthanasia. In some cases patients are not being fed or hydrated by artificial means, and so this alternative would require withholding ordinary food and water from an initially conscious patient.[14] There are, for good reasons, strong social and moral inhibitions to doing this, but even when it is possible it may not be seen merely as forgoing life-sustaining treatment but instead as killing the patient. Doing so in some cases would also result in suffering to the patient until consciousness is lost after about a week. This additional suffering would sometimes attend the withdrawal of artificially provided nutrition and hydration as well. In some cases, the cost of restricting the steps that can be taken in order to hasten death to forgoing of life-support would be a substantially worse death for the patient. The issue should not be whether we can find a treatment to forgo so as to avoid the need for assisted suicide or euthanasia but which means of hastening death will result in the death that is most humane and most in accord with what the patient wants.

Should physicians take part in assisted suicide or euthanasia?

Finally, I want to consider an objection to assisted suicide or euthanasia that is specifically to *physicians* ever performing them. Permitting physicians to perform assisted suicide or euthanasia, it is said, would be incompatible with their fundamental moral and professional commitment as healers to care for patients and to protect life. Moreover, if assisted suicide or euthanasia by physicians became common, patients would come to fear that a medication was intended not to treat or care but instead to kill and would thus lose trust in their physicians. This position was forcefully stated in the paper cited earlier by four prominent physicians and bioethicists:

> The very soul of medicine is on trial. . . . This issue touches medicine at its moral center; if this moral center collapses, if physicians become killers or are even licensed to kill, the

profession—and, therewith, each physician—will never again be worthy of trust and respect as healer and comforter and protector of life in all its frailty.[15]

These authors go on to make clear that while they oppose permitting anyone to perform assisted suicide or euthanasia, their special concern is with physicians' doing so:

We call on fellow physicians to say that they will not deliberately kill. We must also say to each of our fellow physicians that we will not tolerate killing of patients and that we shall take disciplinary action against doctors who kill. And we must say to the broader community that if it insists on tolerating or legalizing active euthanasia, it will have to find nonphysicians to do its killing.[16]

If permitting physicians to kill would undermine the very "moral center" of medicine, then almost certainly physicians should not be permitted to perform assisted suicide or euthanasia. But how persuasive is this claim? Patients should not fear, as a consequence of permitting *voluntary* assisted suicide or euthanasia, that their physicians will substitute a lethal injection for what patients want and believe is part of their care. If assisted suicide and euthanasia are restricted to cases in which they are truly voluntary, then no patient should fear getting either unless he or she has voluntarily requested them. Moreover, the central concern of patients to control their care when dying that has driven the debates over life-sustaining treatment decisions, the development of advance directives, and now assisted suicide and euthanasia, casts further doubt on this purported erosion of patients' trust of their physicians. The fear of loss of control should be lessened, not strengthened, if assisted suicide and euthanasia are permitted. Doing so would extend to dying patients control over their own dying in circumstances where there is no life-sustaining treatment to be withheld or withdrawn, or where waiting for death from forgoing treatment will provide the patient with a substantially worse death.

Might Gaylin and his colleagues, nevertheless, be correct in their claim that the moral center of medicine would collapse if physicians were to become killers? This question raises what at the deepest level should be the guiding aims of medicine, a question that obviously cannot be fully explored here. But I do want to say enough to indicate the direction that I believe an appropriate response to this challenge should take. In spelling out what I called the positive argument for assisted suicide and euthanasia, I suggested that two principal values—respecting patients' self-determination and promoting their well-being—underlie the consensus that competent patients or the surrogates of incompetent patients are entitled to refuse any life-sustaining treatment and to choose from among available alternative treatments. It is the commitment to these two values in guiding physicians' actions as healers, comforters, and protectors of their patients' lives that should be at the "moral center" of medicine, and these two values *support* physicians' performance of assisted suicide or euthanasia when their patients make competent requests for them.

What should not be at that moral center is a commitment to preserving patients' lives as such without regard to whether those patients want their lives preserved or judge their preservation a benefit to them. In recent years, vitalism has been increasingly rejected by physicians and, despite some statements that suggest it, is almost certainly not what Gaylin and colleagues intended. One of them, Leon Kass, has elaborated elsewhere the view that medicine is a moral profession whose proper aim is "the naturally given end of health," understood as the wholeness and well-working of the human being; "for the physician, at least, human life in living bodies commands respect and reverence—*by its very nature.*"[17] Kass continues, "the deepest ethical principle restraining the physician's power is not the autonomy or freedom of the patient; neither is it his own compassion or good intention. Rather, it is the dignity and mysterious power of human life itself."[18] I believe Kass is in the end mistaken about the proper account of the aims of medicine and the limits on physicians' power, but this difficult issue will certainly be one of the central themes in the continuing debate about physicians' roles in assisted suicide and euthanasia.

Restrict assisted suicide to physicians

It is worth adding in conclusion that there are at least three reasons for restricting the performance of assisted suicide or euthanasia to physicians only. First, physicians would inevitably be involved in some of the important procedural safeguards necessary to a defensible practice of assisted suicide or euthanasia, such as ensuring that the patient is well informed about his or her condition, prognosis, and possible treatments and ensuring that all reasonable means have been taken to improve the quality of the patient's life. Second, physicians have access to and knowledge about (or can gain that knowledge with training) the necessary means and methods for carrying out assisted suicide or euthanasia effectively, and so can be instrumental in avoiding failed attempts by the patient to take his or her own life that only worsen the patient's condition. Third, one necessary protection against abuse of any legalization of assisted suicide or euthanasia is to limit who is given authority to perform them so that those persons can be held accountable for their exercise of that authority. Physicians, whose training and professional norms give some assurance that they would perform assisted suicide or euthanasia responsibly, are an appropriate group of persons to whom that authority might be reasonably restricted. But this is to take us beyond the case for which I have argued here, that assisted suicide and euthanasia are morally justified in some individual cases.

Notes

1. This chapter is a substantially revised version of my earlier paper "Voluntary Active Euthanasia," *Hastings Center Report* 22 (March–April 1992): 10–22, which was reprinted in my *Life and Death: Philosophical Essays in Biomedical Ethics* (Cambridge: Cambridge University Press, 1993).

2. Sidney H. Wanzer et al., "The Physician's Responsibility Toward Hopelessly Ill Patients," *New England Journal of Medicine* 310 (1984): 955–59.

3. There is evidence that physicians commonly fail to diagnose depression;

see Robert I. Misbin, "Physicians Aid in Dying," *New England Journal of Medicine* 325 (1991): 1304–7.

4. Anonymous, "It's Over Debbie," *JAMA* 259 (1988): 272.

5. Willard Gaylin et al., "Doctors Must Not Kill," *JAMA* 259 (1988): 2139–40.

6. Bonnie Steinbock and Alastair Norcross, eds., *Killing and Letting Die*, 2d ed. (New York: Fordham University Press, 1994).

7. Dan W. Brock, "Forgoing Food and Water: Is It Killing?" in Joanne Lynn, ed., *By No Extraordinary Means: The Choice to Forgo Life-Sustaining Food and Water* (Bloomington: Indiana University Press, 1986).

8. James Rachels, "Active and Passive Euthanasia," *New England Journal of Medicine* 292 (1975): 78–80; Michael Tooley, *Abortion and Infanticide* (Oxford: Oxford University Press, 1983). In my paper "Taking Human Life," *Ethics* 95 (1985): 851–65, I argue in more detail that killing in itself is not morally different from allowing to die and defend the strategy of argument employed in this paragraph in the text.

9. Dan W. Brock, "Moral Rights and Permissible Killing," in John Ladd, ed., *Ethical Issues Relating to Life and Death* (Oxford: Oxford University Press, 1979).

10. Jeremy Waldron, "A Right to Do Wrong," *Ethics* 92 (1981): 21–39.

11. James Rachels, *The End of Life* (Oxford: Oxford University Press, 1986).

12. Marcia Angell, "The Quality of Mercy," *New England Journal of Medicine* 306 (1982): 98–99; M. Donovan, P. Dillon, and L. Mcguire, "Incidence and Characteristics of Pain in a Sample of Medical-Surgical Inpatients," *Pain* 30 (1987): 69–78.

13. Eric Cassell, *The Nature of Suffering and the Goals of Medicine* (New York: Oxford University Press, 1991).

14. James L. Bernat, Bernard Gert, and R. Peter Mogielnicki, "Patient Refusal of Hydration and Nutrition: An Alternative to Physician-Assisted Suicide or Voluntary Active Euthanasia," *Archives of Internal Medicine* 153 (1993): 2723–28.

15. Gaylin et al.

16. Ibid.

17. Leon R. Kass, "Neither for Love nor Money: Why Doctors Must Not Kill," *Public Interest* 94 (1989): 25–46; see also his *Toward a More Natural Science: Biology and Human Affairs* (New York: Free Press, 1985) chaps. 6–9.

18. Kass, "Neither for Love nor Money," p. 38.

2

Physician-Assisted Suicide Is Not Ethical

James K. Boehnlein

James K. Boehnlein is associate professor of psychiatry and assistant dean for curriculum at Oregon Health Science University.

The act of physician-assisted suicide is inconsistent with the physician's role as healer. If physician-assisted suicide becomes a routine option, the responsibility of the doctor to assist patients at the end of their lives will be diminished. Societal acceptance of physician-assisted suicide will not increase patients' autonomy, as supporters claim. Rather, patients will be pressured in subtle ways by doctors, family members, and a cost-conscious health care system to end their lives prematurely. The ethical role of physicians is to help patients heal, not to hasten their deaths.

P hysician-assisted suicide (PAS) is a complex issue that strikes a chord across all segments of society and throughout medicine and allied fields. It involves discussion and debate about a number of central issues in medicine such as the meaning of professional identity, the doctor/patient relationship and the physician's role in society. Other realities in this current era that mold and shape the debate include continuing advances in medical technology that lengthen life, evolving changes in medical economics that influence the process of medical decision making, and tension at the interface of law and medicine.

Polarization within the medical community largely arises from the fact that physicians on both sides of the issue view the compassionate role of the physician in helping to relieve pain and suffering in entirely different ways. After several years of intense thought and discussion I personally think that the arguments opposed to the active role of physicians in assisted suicide far outweigh arguments that support a physician role. I will use the term "physician-assisted suicide" in this discussion rather than the recently popularized term "physician aid in dying" because I believe the latter term is a euphemism that obscures the true nature of the act under consideration. The term physician aid in dying, as it currently and incorrectly is being used in the medical and popular literature, is ultimately physician aid in death, and is truly physician-assisted suicide. Life is purposefully artificially terminated during the process of dying. True physician aid in dying is the facilitation of a patient's encounter with the natural process of dying, using the bio-psychosocial [biological, psychological, and social] perspectives and skills of the medical profession to nurture, comfort, relieve pain, and provide hope and interpersonal contact.

The arguments against physician-assisted suicide that I will discuss in some detail fall into the following categories: personal autonomy vs. social imperatives; the historical and social role of physicians as instruments of healing; historical precedents for physician-assisted suicide and euthanasia; and, medical economics. It is important to note that in this paper I am not debating the ethically acceptable withdrawal of life sustaining treatment when prolonging life and alleviating suffering are in conflict, nor am I debating the acceptability of the ethical principle of double effect (i.e. using treatment, such as pain medication, to relieve discomfort even when the intervention carries a risk of hastening death, provided the intent is not to end the patient's life).

Personal autonomy vs. social imperatives

Most of the social and legal debate concerning physician-assisted suicide has centered around the issue of individual autonomy and choice over when to end one's own life. These are treasured American values that are at the core of initiatives to legalize physician-assisted suicide. Although I strongly support the ability and right of each individual to make informed medical choices in the great majority of situations, in the specific case of physician-assisted suicide I believe that the adverse effects on society at large outweigh the argument for personal autonomy. Individual choices have implications for other terminally ill patients and for social policy. These broader social factors that include historical and economic perspectives will be discussed in later sections of this paper.

> *The arguments opposed to the active role of physicians in assisted suicide far outweigh arguments that support a physician role.*

I believe that the argument emphasizing the primacy of personal autonomy creates a false dichotomy that unnecessarily polarizes current discussions of physician-assisted suicide. The process of PAS is not truly autonomous in the first place because it involves the interpersonal dynamics of the doctor/patient relationship, and the dying patient's relationship with friends and family. There can be unconscious coercion by family members or care providers, including the tendency to choose irreversible actions, including suicide, when faced with the helplessness experienced in the face of death. Depressed patients may attempt to convince their provider of the worthlessness and hopelessness of their lives, and the potential impairment of their autonomy may be forgotten

(Ganzini & Lee, 1997). All people, doctors and patients alike, are consciously and unconsciously influenced by others, and develop and maintain their sense of being valuable through relationships with others (Hamilton, Edwards, Boehnlein, et al, 1998). Subtle, coercive communication (New York State Task Force, 1994) can be powerful; some patients may even experience mention of assisted suicide as suggestion, lack of therapeutic hope, or an assertion that their life is no longer worthwhile.

Although PAS is viewed currently as a patient's autonomous decision and exercise of personal choice, in reality the balance of power lies with the physician. The individual's option to request a physician's aid in hastening death could too easily become a duty to request that aid. Broad legalization of physician-assisted suicide and euthanasia would have the paradoxical effect of making patients seem to be responsible for their own suffering; rather than being seen primarily as the victims of pain and suffering caused by disease, patients would be seen as having the power to end their suffering by agreeing to an injection or taking pills, and refusing would mean that living through the pain was the patient's decision, the patient's responsibility (Emanuel 1996, 1997). Furthermore, shifting the responsibility for the decision to the patient in a covert manner (but ultimately maintaining the real and symbolic power of the prescription pad) may also decrease the motivation of caregivers to provide extra care. In the long run, this further contributes to the ambivalence of the public towards physicians regarding power, control and responsibility, particularly when there are financial conflicts of interest in continuing care.

Medical ethics through history

The clinical choices faced by physicians have become increasingly more complex because of the development of modern medical technology and the wider scope of medical activities (Kunstadter, 1980). In traditional non-Western world cultures, there is an acceptance of mortality, and death is considered a part of the human condition (Parkes, Laungani & Young, 1997). Medical healers are viewed with trust and respect, and with the explicit expectation that the physician will treat illness and preserve life. In a disturbing number of societies, however, medical knowledge and procedures have been used specifically and primarily to terminate life. In each example, medical ethics become relative and partially dependent upon social and governmental needs at the time.

For example, Lifton (1986) in his comprehensive description of the central role of physicians during the Nazi genocide, notes that not only were physicians acting as technicians in the development and implementation of lethal injection and euthanasia, but they were also intellectual and moral leaders in the Nazi state's medicalization of killing. Psychiatrists, in particular, were used as gatekeepers in assessing the competency and quality of life of mentally impaired persons thought to be candidates for lethal injection; in an ironic twist that chillingly prefigures supposedly protective safeguards in contemporary proposals for physician-assisted suicide, accuracy of diagnosis and quality assurance were felt to be guaranteed by the second opinion of another physician. Any reservations could be overcome by the convening of a medical committee, that is, by keeping the procedure medicalized. Lifton further notes that state-sanctioned euthanasia came to be viewed by layman and physician alike as a form of "therapy" and became an "ethical" course of action.

It is important to note that this evolution of thinking in the German legal and medical community began insidiously as early as 1920 with the publication of "The Permission to Destroy Life Unworthy of Life" by Karl Binding, a jurist, and Alfred Hocke, a psychiatrist (Lifton, 1986). The authors professionalized and medicalized the process, describing the doctor's legal responsibility in "death assistance" of the incurably ill, the mentally ill and the mentally retarded. Again prefiguring contemporary laws legalizing PAS, a carefully controlled process was advocated, with applications for killing evaluated by a three-person panel (a general physician, a psychiatrist, and a lawyer). A consenting patient would have the right to withdraw that consent at any time, and there also was an emphasis on the legal protection of physicians involved in the killing process; both of these provisions also are included in the Oregon Death With Dignity Act approved by Oregon voters in 1994 and 1997.

> *Although physician-assisted suicide is viewed currently as a patient's autonomous decision and exercise of personal choice, in reality the balance of power lies with the physician.*

Like PAS and euthanasia, another contemporary example of the socially-sanctioned inappropriate use of medical technology and expertise is lethal injection of condemned prisoners. Society attempts to expand executions by cloaking them in a medical aura (Bolsen, 1982); executions by lethal injection, carried out in a quasimedical setting, give the impression that a medical procedure is being administered (Trent, 1986). In fact the physician is using knowledge and skills attained during medical education and is thus recognized by society as possessing and using those specific skills that are normally used to sustain and enhance life (Boehnlein et al, 1995). As with PAS, society uses the medical profession and the socially sanctioned skills of the profession to legitimize killing to help solve a social problem and to minimize public expenditure. In fact, shortly after the Oregon Death With Dignity law was reaffirmed in November, 1997, the State of Oregon proposed that physician-assisted suicide be added to the list of "medical procedures" covered by the Oregon Health Plan, the state's health plan for the poor. The state's argument in support of physician-assisted suicide is that "this is a medical procedure authorized by the voters of Oregon . . . we want to make sure our agencies recognize it as a medical procedure" (O'Neill, 1997). We are, at once, entering a new era in which acceptable "medical procedures" are absurdly determined by majority popular vote and revisiting a dangerous ethical and moral conflict of interest in which the state can hasten the death of its citizens, particularly the poor, when keeping them alive with a terminal illness may prove too costly. This is an excellent example of how illogical and irrelevant it is to label philosophical positions on this issue as being either "conservative" or "liberal". A specific political philosophy, in fact, may influence positions on either side of this complex issue.

As with the medicalization of capital punishment in the United States, the use of the prescription pad or lethal injection to hasten death in terminally ill patients is an inappropriate use of medical knowledge and technology, reducing the moral stature of the medical profession in both symbolic and realistic ways. Physicians are no longer viewed exclusively as healers and as unambivalent patient advocates. It is ironic that the more advances are made in science, the more there is fear and denial of the reality of death (Kübler-Ross, 1969). Physicians traditionally have not been adequately trained in how to talk with dying patients—their fears, their reflections on the meaning of their lives, their regrets. Because it is difficult and exhausting work, it may be easier for the doctor, given the option, to avoid this type of discussion by writing a prescription for life ending medication. The process of writing a lethal prescription further marginalizes and isolates the dying patient, and protects the doctor; he or she is not required to be there at the time of ingestion and does not have to witness directly the ultimate consequences of writing the lethal prescription. It diminishes the responsibility of the physician and the medical profession to assist the patient in the process of dying. Moreover, legalizing physician-assisted suicide by oral ingestion of medication legitimizes a medical procedure for which there is virtually no research. In fact, the presumption of an early death easily contributes to an atmosphere in which indirect medical experimentation is permitted without the usual safeguards that have been instituted in recent decades when new medical procedures or medications have been developed in clinical trials. This lack of proper oversight of what is, in reality, an experimental procedure further contributes to the indignity of the dying individual.

The role of the psychiatrist

Of all medical specialists, psychiatrists are the best trained in observing human behavior and assessing the motivations and consequences of behavior. There can be both unconscious and conscious motivations for any behavior, particularly behavior that has life and death implications. Transference and countertransference add even more variables to the complexities of physician-assisted suicide. [Transference is a term for feelings and desires that a patient has toward a therapist; countertransference refers to the feelings a therapist has toward the patient.]

Transference issues involved in choosing physician-assisted suicide include the patient's need to please others or to diminish the suffering of those they love or respect who are watching them die. The psychiatrist's countertransference can be exhibited in a number of ways, including the desire to exert power and control over death, or unconsciously encouraging the patient's consideration of PAS in order to relieve the emotional suffering associated with watching a patient die, although on a conscious level it would appear that the psychiatrist is facilitating patient autonomy and relief of suffering. Also, as physicians and psychiatrists, we do not want to judge ourselves, or be judged by others, as being callous to patient suffering. On a personal level this would be seen as inhumane, on a professional level as unethical. Yet, as psychiatrists we are also trained to be aware of the potential difference between an expressed wish for death and the underlying wish for interpersonal human contact, comfort and support, and the validation that one's life is valuable despite a decline in activity level, physical appearance or role performance in family or society. And as Bowlby (1973, 1977), Yalom (1980) and others have eloquently described, the anticipation or actual experience of abandonment by others is one of the most painful of all human experiences.

The use of the prescription pad or lethal injection to hasten death in terminally ill patients is an inappropriate use of medical knowledge.

Another issue particularly germaine to the psychiatrist's role is the actual assessment of a patient's judgment and competency to commit suicide. There are absolutely no professional standards to judge competency for suicide. Moreover, it is particularly ironic that in our education and training we are carefully taught to assess risk factors for suicide, to screen for psychiatric problems that may precipitate suicide, and to intervene to prevent suicide. Not only is this standard ethical psychiatric practice, but we can be sued if we do not take appropriate steps to screen for, or prevent, suicide. With PAS, the tables are inappropriately turned to the position that a physician's assistance in ending life is judged to be the ethical course of action; active and intentional enhancement of the dying process by the physician's knowledge and skills is judged to be the appropriate "therapy" to relieve illness and suffering.

The primary focus on patient autonomy in debates promoting PAS also undermines a more systems view of human behavior and optimal mental health that finally has become more prominent in psychiatric theory and treatment in the past two decades. PAS laws that discourage or prohibit family awareness of choices related to the suicidal act are an antiquated throwback to theoretical concepts of personal identity, motivation and behavior that conceptualize individuals as living in a vacuum, uninfluenced by others and not influencing others. And, as psychiatrists, we are particularly aware of the devastating effect of suicide upon generations of surviving family members. The suicidal act does not occur in isolation.

Implications of cost control

The current debate about the ethics of physician-assisted suicide is occurring at the same time that there are major changes in the way health care in the United States is being delivered and financed. In the era of managed care, there are increasing incentives for doctors and health care organizations to limit the amount of medical care that is delivered. These incentives for cost control have major implications for decisions made by physicians, along with patients and their families, at the end of life.

Since comprehensive care for dying patients is not universally available in the United States, patients and their families can face painful decisions about whether or not one week or one month more of expensive medical care is truly worthwhile, or whether that money is best spent on younger surviving generations of the family. In the Netherlands, where physician-assisted suicide is widely accepted and practiced, there has been an erosion of medical standards in the care of terminally ill patients, and there is inadequate training of physicians in palliative care (Hendin et al, 1997).

These decisions raise many subjective considerations about the quality of individual lives that can be subtly influenced by realistic fears of financial ruin or a belief that self-sacrifice will make life easier financially and emotionally for surviving generations. As mentioned earlier, a right to die can easily evolve into a duty to die. This decision making process can be complicated further by the influence of the health care team, whose unconscious motives may not be completely altruistic when there may be financial benefits associated with an earlier death hastened by physician-assisted suicide. Physicians depend on role clarity and clear boundaries to guide them; adding assisted-suicide to the social role of physicians insolubly confuses this role clarity. It is ironic that in an era in which there is greatly increased emphasis on quality assurance in medical care, proposals for implementing the practice of PAS, with an emphasis on secretiveness and minimal professional monitoring, go in the opposite direction. Again, this further marginalizes the dying process and mutes debate about the role of physicians in society.

Physician as healer

As I have argued, there are too many historical, social and economic arguments against PAS to allow it as an acceptable and ethical professional practice. These arguments, throughout diverse cultures and historical eras, are not exclusively or primarily religious ones, as supporters of PAS frequently argue. Instead, they are carefully formed perspectives that have been developed in the major philosophies of the East and West over millenia, drawing upon social and historical experience. Religion, whether it is Islam, Judaism, Christianity, Hinduism, or Buddhism, infuses the social fabric of the major cultures of the world, and it is inseparably linked with secular traditions of medicine and healing. To artificially separate out and criticize certain arguments against PAS as "religious" is to, more accurately, criticize much of the foundation of healing traditions of East and West.

As physicians and psychiatrists, we do not want to judge ourselves, or be judged by others, as being callous to patient suffering. On a personal level this would be seen as inhumane, on a professional level as unethical.

Actions performed by a physician with the implicit purpose of causing the death of the patient would alter the trust and longstanding universal role of the physician as healer. The intent of the physician is vitally important. Intent is not only a philosophical issue, but it can affect clinical judgment and outcome. When death is even considered as a form of "treatment," then the context of all treatment options is reframed to the extent that PAS will be progressively considered as an option earlier in treatment and in a broader range of cases. That the majority of psychiatrists in the Netherlands endorse PAS for intractable mental disorders (Groenewoud, et al, 1997) suggests that beliefs about what is permissible expand as a result of acculturation to changes in social policy (Ganzini & Lee, 1997). In the Netherlands the persistence of abuse and the violation of safeguards to protect children and the mentally ill, despite publicity and condemnation, suggest that the feared consequences of legalization are exactly its inherent consequences; the future confluence of ethical arguments, accepted medical practice, demographic and budgetary pressures, and a social ethos that views the old and sick as burdens could overwhelm any barriers against euthanasia even for incompetent patients (Emanuel, 1997).

There are too many historical, social and economic arguments against physician-assisted suicide to allow it as an acceptable and ethical professional practice.

In order for true ethical decision making to occur in medicine, the physician needs to be aware continually of how his or her role, as healer and physician, is defined by society at any given time. When confronted with contemporary concrete ethical problems, such as physician-assisted suicide, the physician must be able to draw upon a broadly based intellectual tradition not only in the biological sciences but also in the humanities and social sciences. It is essential for clinicians to have a broad historical perspective on the development of their profession's standards and values in order to deal effectively with current or future ethical dilemmas. For contemporary physicians, the challenge is to continue to explore and critically question the foundations of their personal and professional values throughout their career.

The ethics of PAS will continue to be debated in society for decades to come. Strongly held, coherent, and persuasive opinions will be expressed by representatives on all sides of the issue. Yet, my own personal opinions about PAS continue to be grounded in the historical and social determinants explained earlier; in the belief that a truly dignified death does not come at the hand of a physician-healer despite compelling arguments that it is a compassionate act; and finally, my continued belief that when individuals cannot make conscious, rational, autonomous choices, their human dignity still is not lessened.

References

Boehnlein, J.K., Parker, R.M., Arnold, R.M., Bosk, C.F., & Sparr, L.F. (1995). Medical ethics, cultural values, and physician participation in lethal injection. Bulletin of the American Academy of Psychiatry and the Law, 23, 129–134.

Bolsen, B. (1982). Strange bedfellows: Death penalty and medicine. Journal of the American Medical Association, 248, 518–519.

Bowlby, J. (1973). Attachment and Loss, vol. 2: Separation. New York: Basic-Books.

Bowlby, J. (1977). The making and breaking of affectional bonds. British Journal of Psychiatry, 130, 201–218.

Emanuel, E.J., Fairclough, D.L., Daniels, E.R., & Clarridge, B.R. (1996). Euthanasia and physician-assisted suicide: Attitudes and experiences of oncology patients, oncologists, and the public. Lancet, 347, 1805–1810.

Emanuel, E.J. (1997). Who's right to die? The Atlantic Monthly, 279(3), 73–79.

Ganzini, L. & Lee, M.A. (1997). Psychiatry and assisted suicide in the United States. New England Journal of Medicine, 336, 1824–1826.

Groenewoud, J.H., van der Maas, P.J., van der Wal, G., Hengeveld, M.W., Tholen, A.J., Schudel, W.J., & van der Heide, A. (1997). Physician-assisted death in psychiatric practice in the Netherlands. New England Journal of Medicine, 336, 1795–1801.

Hamilton, N.G., Edwards, P.J., Boehnlein, J.K., & Hamilton, C.A. (1998). The doctor-patient relationship and physician-assisted suicide: A contribution from dynamic psychiatry. American Journal of Forensic Psychiatry, 19, 59–75.

Hendin, H., Rutenfrans, C., & Zylicz, Z. (1997). Physician-assisted suicide and euthanasia in the Netherlands: Lessons from the Dutch. Journal of the American Medical Association, 277, 1720–1722.

Kübler-Ross, E. (1969). On Death and Dying. New York: Macmillan.

Kunstadter, P. (1980). Medical ethics in cross-cultural and multi-cultural perspectives. Social Science and Medicine, 14B, 289–298.

Lifton, R.J. (1986). The Nazi Doctors: Medical Killing and the Psychology of Genocide. New York: BasicBooks.

New York State Task Force on Life and the Law. (1994). When death is sought: Assisted suicide and euthanasia in the medical context. Albany, NY: Health Education Services.

O'Neill, P. (1997). Suicide, gender raise questions for health plan. The Oregonian, December 11, 1997.

Parkes, C.M., Laungani, P., & Young, B. (Eds.). (1997). Death and Bereavement Across Cultures. London: Routledge.

Trent, B. (1986). Capital punishment: MD politicians share their views. Canadian Medical Association Journal, 143, 792–798.

Yalom, I.D. (1980). Existential Psychotherapy. New York: BasicBooks.

3

Access to Physician-Assisted Suicide Is an Unalienable Right

Andrew Lewis

Andrew Lewis hosts his own radio show and sits on the board of contributors of the Intellectual Activist, *a monthly review of current events and books.*

The U.S. Constitution protects an individual's right to decide how to live and how to die. Consequently, those who seek to make physician-assisted suicide legal or illegal ignore the implicit constitutionality of this right. Republicans who oppose physician-assisted suicide want the federal government to violate the Constitution by making physician-assisted suicide illegal. Even Democratic supporters of physician-assisted suicide deny its implicit constitutionality by encouraging the government to regulate its practice.

In 1994, 51% of Oregon's voters supported the "Death with Dignity Act," and 60% reaffirmed it in 1997. The law recognized the right of terminally ill patients to end their suffering legally and painlessly by allowing a doctor to prescribe a lethal dose of medication upon request. Two doctors must deem the patient—who must be an adult—to be terminally ill and mentally competent, he must be informed of all options for alleviating his suffering, and the doctor must observe a 15-day waiting period between the decision and the prescription. In 1998, the first full year of the law's operation, 15 people used the law to end their lives by lethal prescription. A further six were recognized as eligible but died from their illnesses before they could take the medication. In 1999, approximately 20 people ended their lives with a physician's assistance.

Now, however, the Oregon law—and the right to assisted suicide—is under attack by religious conservatives. While the battlefield is Oregon's law and the right to die, the real war is over the right to live.

The Supreme Court has failed to acknowledge a constitutional right to medically-assisted suicide. In the same year that Oregonians reaffirmed their support for the Death with Dignity Act, the Court abstained from its responsibility and deemed the issue a matter for individual states to decide.

To circumvent Oregon's law and the Supreme Court's buck-passing, the House of Representatives voted in November 1999 to amend the 1970 Federal Controlled Substances Act to prohibit the use of drugs for anything other than palliative care, i.e., pain relief. Republicans, usually staunch advocates of "states' rights" against federal power, surrendered their own political principles to their religious prejudice against assisted suicide.

Your right to control your own life . . . is yours your entire adult life, up to and including the time and manner of your death.

The "Pain Relief Promotion Act" effectively places federal drug agents in the treatment room to monitor doctors' activities. Pain-relieving drugs, such as morphine, have multiple uses and effects. While they alleviate pain, they can also hasten death. Highly trained doctors who know the effects of such drugs and can prescribe them appropriately—whatever their intent—will now be second-guessed by federal police agents who will have the authority to determine what the physician's purpose was. If one of these medical cops deems that a doctor has prescribed a drug "for the purpose of causing death," that doctor faces up to 20 years in jail.

(The bill's passage through the Senate is uncertain. Debate has been postponed until the spring of 2000, where it will be opposed, chiefly by Oregon senator Ron Wyden. President Bill Clinton is generally opposed to physician-assisted suicide but has yet to make a statement about this legislation.)[*]

More important, the new law directly violates a basic freedom which is, in fact, neither a matter for the Supreme Court to leave in the hands of the states nor for the states to leave up to the voters. As the right to abortion follows from the basic principle of individual rights, so too does the right to end one's own life, and the right to request assistance in ending it. The central issue is not the right to end your life, but the right to live and enjoy it.

The right to assisted suicide

The principle of individual rights means the right to direct the course of your entire life, to take those actions that you judge necessary for your life and happiness. The rights to life, liberty, and the pursuit of happiness are inseparable. They mean the right to live for the sake of your values and your enjoyment of them. If you determine that it is no longer possible to achieve your values, that all you face is misery, no one may force you to act in defiance of that judgment. Your right to control your own life, to set the terms of your own existence, is yours your entire adult life, up to and including the time and manner of your death.

---

[*] The Pain Relief Promotion Act had not passed in the Senate as of August 2001.

To concretize the meaning of this right, let us examine one actual case. Early in 1999 Patrick, a 43-year-old craftsman almost completely paralyzed from Lou Gehrig's disease, strapped a computer mouse to his foot and tapped out a goodbye note—the only means left to him to communicate with others. He printed the note for his parents, paid his funeral expenses, then retreated to his trailer and, with the aide of his brother-in-law, swallowed a chocolate drink laced with 90 capsules of doctor-prescribed barbiturates to end his own life.

The right to physician-assisted suicide is an inalienable, individual right, which should be recognized throughout the country.

What would be the point of denying Patrick the right to pursue this option? The only end that can be achieved would be to force him to suffer through an existence that has become hateful to him. Yet that is precisely what opponents of the right to die want to do.

In essence, opponents of assisted suicide believe that the individual has no rights at all—that rights are no more than a permit issued by a reluctant God or forbearing state which maintains ultimate sanction over the individual's life and death. Life, they hold, is a duty to be endured at the price of any suffering, and the greater the suffering the greater the glory.

Drawing inspiration from the Bible ("He that loveth his life shall lose it, and he that hateth his life in this world shall keep it unto life eternal."[1]) and from [philosopher] Immanuel Kant (". . . if adversity and hopeless sorrow have completely taken away the relish for life; if the unfortunate one, strong in mind, indignant at his fate rather than despondent or dejected, wishes for death, and yet preserves his life without loving it—not from inclination or fear, but from duty—then his [action] has a moral worth."[2]), they wish to make life a living hell of unchosen obligations and servitude. Just as they would impose on every woman the prospect of a lifelong burden of parenthood (by outlawing abortion), so they seek to impose on the terminally ill a burden of senseless suffering.

Tragically, however, the same basic philosophic premise is shared by assisted suicide's leading *supporters*.

By and large, these supporters are modern liberals—pragmatic socialists —who claim your life belongs to the state, not to God. They believe they have the right to tax you to death in the first place, but they will then allow you to appeal to special circumstances and pity to make only one crucial choice on your own terms. This relativistic standard leaves the state with total control over how (and when) you may live and is no protection at all for the right to die they claim to uphold.

Whatever the rationalization, it is against free will, independence, and happiness that the opponents and supporters are united. Individuals such as Patrick are solemnly condemned to a life of suffering without hope or reason for living.

In *every* decision of a man's life, he must be free to follow his own moral convictions. Choosing the manner of his death is merely an extension of his right to determine the course of his life. Oregonians recognized this principle and acted courageously to affirm it. The right to physician-assisted suicide is an inalienable, individual right, which should be recognized throughout the country, not merely because it is consistent with the principles stated in the Constitution, but because it is an inescapable expression of liberty.

The right to the pursuit of happiness, so carefully worded by Thomas Jefferson and the Founding Fathers, means the right to set the goals and terms of your own existence. Recognizing the right of Patrick and many others to end their own lives means more than respecting their autonomy; it means affirming the right of each man to pursue his own happiness.

References

1. The Bible, John 12:25.

2. Immanuel Kant, *Groundwork for the Metaphysics of Morals,* Section 1, in *The Philosophy of Kant,* translated & edited by Carl J. Friedrich (The Modern Library, 1977), p. 145.

Physician-Assisted Suicide Should Not Be Legalized

Wesley J. Smith

Wesley J. Smith is an attorney for the International Anti-Euthanasia Task Force. He is the author of Culture of Death: The Destruction of Medical Ethics in America.

The experience of Oregon and the Netherlands, where assisted suicide is legal, reveals that legalizing suicide is a mistake. Once the practice is made legal, some physicians circumvent guidelines designed to protect vulnerable patients, while some patients search for a doctor who will issue a prescription for a lethal dose of medication. In addition, pressure to cut medical costs threatens to make assisted suicide more common as an alternative to prolonged medical care.

In November 1999, Congress took up the issues of pain control and physician-assisted suicide, with the House voting 271–156 to pass the Pain Relief Promotion Act. The legislation, if passed, would improve pain control while deterring physician-assisted suicide. Doctors who prescribe lethal drugs for the purpose of killing their terminally ill patients would be subject to losing their federal licenses to prescribe. [This bill did not pass.]

On the floor of the House and in comments to media, supporters of the bill referred specifically to the example of Oregon, where assisted suicide is legal. They were right to do so. Oregon's assisted suicide law continues to demonstrate that permitting doctors to help kill patients is bad medicine and even worse public policy.

The most recent assisted suicide in Oregon is a case in point. On October 17, 1999, the *Oregonian* published an account of one patient who committed suicide with the assistance of medical professionals. The patient's family had provided the newspaper with the details of the assisted killing, unintentionally showing how Oregon's law endangers those who are the least capable of defending themselves.

Kate Cheney, age 85, was diagnosed with terminal cancer and wanted assisted suicide, but there was a problem. She may have had dementia, which raised questions of mental competence. So, rather than prescribe lethal drugs, her doctor referred her to a psychiatrist, as required by law.

Cheney was accompanied to the consultation by her daughter, Erika Goldstein. The psychiatrist found that Cheney had a loss of short-term memory. Even more worrisome, it appeared that her daughter had more of a vested interest in Cheney's assisted suicide than did Cheney herself. The psychiatrist wrote in his report that while the assisted suicide seemed consistent with Cheney's values, "she does not seem to be explicitly pushing for this." He also determined that she did not have the "very high capacity required to weigh options about assisted suicide." Accordingly, he nixed the assisted suicide.

Advocates of legalization might, at this point, smile happily and point out that such refusals are part of the way the law operates. But that isn't the end of Kate Cheney's story. According to the *Oregonian*, Cheney appeared to accept the psychiatrist's verdict, but her daughter did not. Goldstein viewed the guidelines protecting her mother's life as obstacles, a "road-block" to Cheney's right to die. So, she shopped for another doctor.

Oregon's assisted suicide law continues to demonstrate that permitting doctors to help kill patients is bad medicine and even worse public policy.

Goldstein's demand for a second opinion was acceded to by Kaiser Permanente, Cheney's HMO. This time a clinical psychologist rather than an MD-psychiatrist examined her. Like the first doctor, the psychologist found Cheney had memory problems. For example, she could not recall when she had been diagnosed with terminal cancer. The psychologist also worried about familial pressure, writing that Cheney's decision to die "may be influenced by her family's wishes." Still, despite these reservations, the psychologist determined that Cheney was competent to kill herself and approved the writing of the lethal prescription.

The final decision was left to an ethicist/administrator who works for Kaiser named Robert Richardson. Dr. Richardson interviewed Cheney, who told him she wanted the pills not because she was in irremediable pain but because she feared not being able to attend to her personal hygiene. After the interview, satisfied that she was competent, Richardson gave the okay for the assisted killing.

Cheney did not take the pills right away. At one point, she asked to die when her daughter had to help her shower after an accident with her colostomy bag, but she quickly changed her mind. Then, Cheney went into a nursing home for a week so that her family could have some respite from care giving. The time in the nursing home seemed to have pushed Cheney into wanting immediate death. As soon as she returned home, she declared her desire to take the pills. After grandchildren were called to say their goodbyes, Cheney took the poison. She died with her daughter at her side, telling her what a courageous woman she was.

This sad story illustrates many profound and unsettling truths about assisted suicide:

Protective guidelines don't protect. Once the legal view of killing is shifted from automatically bad to possibly good, it becomes virtually impossible to restrict physician-assisted suicide to the very narrow range of patients for whom proponents claim it is reserved. The "protective guidelines" allegedly designed to guard the lives of vulnerable people soon become scorned as obstacles to be circumvented. And so, eligibility for physician-assisted suicide steadily expands to permit the killing of increasing categories of ill and disabled patients. Thus, an act that is supposed to be "rare" is likely to become more common. And what was seen as a last resort, something that might be considered if palliative treatment failed, becomes an alternative to treatment.

The Dutch law is a failure

This has certainly happened in the Netherlands, where euthanasia has been permitted since 1973. The Dutch law, in fact, contains much stronger guidelines than Oregon's, yet these protections have long ceased to be of any practical use and are routinely ignored with impunity. Thus, in the Netherlands, not only are terminally ill patients who ask for euthanasia killed by doctors, but so are chronically ill patients, and depressed patients who have no disease. Babies born with disabilities are also killed at the request of parents who allege their children are incapable of a "livable life."

According to repeated reports on Dutch euthanasia, at least 1,000 patients are killed each year who did not ask to die. At the same time, 59 percent of the doctors who kill patients fail to report them as required by the guidelines. One recent study of the Dutch experience puts the matter grimly, saying physician-assisted suicide is "beyond effective control."

The same pattern is already developing in Oregon, where assisted suicide has only been permitted legally for two years. Rather than being strictly reserved for the rare case of irremediable pain, as Oregon voters were told it would be when they legalized the practice, it turns out that none of the patients reported to have undergone assisted suicide were in untreatable agony. Most, like Kate Cheney, were worried about being a burden and requiring assistance with the tasks of daily living. That is a serious problem to be sure, but one which experts on treating dying people are adept at relieving.

According to repeated reports on Dutch euthanasia, at least 1,000 patients are killed each year who did not ask to die.

Doctor-shopping becomes the key to obtaining death. A major selling point of assisted-suicide advocacy is that close personal relationships between doctors and patients will prevent "wrongly decided" assisted suicides. But Oregon proves the utter emptiness of this promise. Kate Cheney and her family were not deterred in the least by a psychiatrist's refusal to approve her self-poisoning. They simply went to another doctor.

Cheney's family wasn't so much looking for a medical opinion as an opinion that confirmed what they had already decided. This is reminiscent of the Woody Allen line from the movie, *Manhattan*. When Allen's character bemoans his marriage breaking up, a friend reminds him that his psychiatrist warned him that his soon-to-be ex-wife would be big trouble. Allen smiles ruefully and says, "Yeah, but she was so pretty, I got another psychiatrist."

Cheney's case is not the only example from Oregon in which doctor-shopping has hastened death. As reported in newspapers and bioethics journals, the first woman known to have legally committed assisted-suicide in Oregon went to her own doctor when her breast cancer prevented her from doing aerobics and gardening. When he refused to help kill her, she consulted a second doctor. This physician also refused to help kill her, diagnosing her as depressed. So, she went to an assisted suicide advocacy group. After speaking on the phone with her, the group's medical director referred her to a "death doctor" who was known to the group for being willing to issue lethal prescriptions. She died a mere two and a half weeks later from the poison pills.

Physician-assisted suicide is not good medicine

According to the *New England Journal of Medicine*, at least five other people who died by assisted suicide in Oregon in 1998 went to multiple physicians before finding one willing to help kill them. The length of time between meeting with the prescribing doctor and death in at least a few cases was 15 days—the exact waiting period required by law. Legalizing assisted suicide thus distorts medical care for patients near the end of their lives.

Primary care physicians who would prefer treating a patient who wants to be killed are jettisoned in favor of doctors with an ideological predisposition toward assisted suicide. Moreover, physician-assisted suicide means doctors who refuse to "assist" are subject to emotional blackmail. Patients can simply tell their physicians: Either you give me the pills or I go to a doctor who will.

Death doctors are a malevolent twist on the draft doctors of the Vietnam war era who kept young men from being inducted by finding physical anomalies to obtain medical deferment for their "patients." But no one pretended that draft doctors were practicing medicine. They were engaged in politics, pure and simple. The same phenomenon is now happening in Oregon, only instead of trying to save lives, death doctors ideologically support the taking of life. This means that even the most secure and long-lasting doctor-patient relationships provide zero protection against assisted suicide.

A lethal part of the mix

HMOs are a lethal part of the mix. One awful truth about assisted suicide is that it will be performed in the context of managed care where profits are made from cutting costs. In Kate Cheney's case, the final authority was a Kaiser HMO medical ethicist. This raises the appearance, if not the actuality, of a terrible conflict of interest. The poison that killed Cheney cost Kaiser approximately $40. It could have cost the HMO $40,000 to care for her properly until her natural death. The potential for economically driven death decisions is too obvious to be denied and is likely to become more pronounced as people become desensitized to doctors' acting as killers. The same can be said about government-financed health care. Oregon Medicaid, which rations health care to the poor, pays for assisted suicide.

Oregon illustrates the danger of redefining killing as a medical act. Yet, despite the warning signs, advocates continue to press legalization throughout the nation. Several states, including California, have legislation pending, while Maine voters faced a legalization initiative in November 2000. The only question is whether we will respond to terminal illness with better medical care, in which case the House vote is a positive sign, or ignore the horrors of the Netherlands and Oregon and step intentionally off of the ethical cliff.

5

Society Favors the Legalization of Physician-Assisted Suicide

Faye Girsh

Faye Girsh is executive director of the Hemlock Society USA, a right-to-die organization based in Denver, Colorado.

There is more interest than ever before in the right of terminally ill patients to end their own lives. Medical science has come a long way in eradicating diseases that kill, so more people are living longer and are not dying suddenly. Therefore, patients are often in great pain and discomfort. For this reason they need to have the option to hasten their own death.

While Americans consider themselves free to live the lives they choose, most don't realize that this freedom ends when it comes to selecting a peaceful death over a life filled with unbearable pain and suffering. Euthanasia advocate Jack Kevorkian's conviction of second-degree murder for assisting in the nationally televised suicide of terminally ill Thomas Youk has shown that, despite achieving great legal successes over the last 25 years, Americans have a long way to go in securing the freedom to die with dignity when confronted by terminal illness.

Interest in the right-to-die issue has become increasingly important as people are now enjoying longer, healthier lives than at any time in history. Diseases that kill suddenly and prematurely have been virtually wiped out in developed countries. What are left are conditions that often result in lingering, agonizing declines—cancer, stroke, Parkinson's disease, and amyotrophic lateral sclerosis (Lou Gehrig's disease), to name a few. Ninety percent of the people who die each year are victims of prolonged illnesses or have experienced a predictable and steady decline due to heart disease, diabetes, or Alzheimer's disease.

Medicine can keep people alive with artificial organs, transplants, and machines—even artificial food and water—rather than allowing a

From "Death with Dignity: Choices and Challenges," by Faye Girsh, *USA Today*, March 2000. Copyright © 2000 by *USA Today Magazine*. Reprinted with permission of the Society for the Advancement of Education.

terminally ill patient a quick death through pneumonia or organ failure. Modern medicine often does more than prolong living—it actually extends dying.

A study of dying patients in five major medical centers revealed that 59% would have preferred to receive just care to make them more comfortable, instead of the aggressive treatment they got. Another study surveyed Canadian patients who identified five areas of importance at the end of life: receiving adequate pain and symptom management; avoiding prolonged dying; achieving a sense of control; relieving the burden on loved ones; and strengthening relationships with people.

A big advancement in caring for terminally ill patients has come with the growth in hospice care, which started with one facility in 1974 and has grown to almost 3,000 nationwide, making it accessible to most Americans. Hospice care is designed to control pain and provide physical and spiritual comfort to those who are dying. It neither prolongs nor hastens death. While hospices have dramatically improved end-of-life care, there remains a serious gap between the choices people want at the end of their lives and what they are now permitted.

Patients' rights at the end of their lives take two forms—the right to refuse medical treatment when faced with inevitable death and the right to secure a doctor's help in ending suffering at the end of life. It took the deaths of two young women—Karen Ann Quinlan and Nancy Cruzan—to give every American the right to make medical decisions in advance. Both had gone into irreversible comas following accidents and, after lengthy legal battles, their parents received permission from the courts to disconnect their daughters' life support.

In Cruzan's case, which took place 14 years after Quinlan's, the Supreme Court ruled that every American has the right to refuse unwanted medical treatment for any reason, even if it leads to death. This includes the right to refuse food and fluids. Justice William Brennan wrote, "Dying is personal. And it is profound. For many, the thought of an ignoble end, steeped in decay, is abhorrent. A quiet, proud death, bodily integrity intact, is a matter of extreme consequence."

Physician-assisted suicide is legal in Oregon

Physician-assisted dying is legal today only in Oregon, where voters legalized the practice in 1994 and again in 1997. During the first year, 23 patients obtained medication from their doctors, but just 15 used it to end their lives. Six others died natural deaths, and two were still living when the study was completed. This shows that people want to know they have a choice, but not all will take advantage of it. Under the provisions of the Oregon Death with Dignity Act:

• The request must come voluntarily from a mentally competent, terminally ill, adult resident of Oregon.

• Two physicians must examine the patient to confirm the diagnosis and prognosis.

• A mental health professional must be consulted if either doctor has a question about mental competence, depression, or coercion.

• All other alternatives must be presented and explained to the patient.

• The patient must make witnessed requests orally and in writing.

• After a 15-day waiting period, the patient receives a physician's prescription for a lethal dose of medication, which can be filled following a two-day waiting period.
• All prescriptions under the Death with Dignity law must be reported to the state health department.
• The patient is then free to take the medication when and if he or she wishes. Family, friends, and a doctor may be present.

Thanks to the laws allowing patients to refuse medical treatment and the growing availability of hospice care, we have more control over how we die. The changes happened because people demanded better care and more options at the end of life. These progressive measures were opposed at first because of the fear of abuse. Naysayers predicted that giving individuals the choice to live or die would lead to a cheapening of human life. Now, though, they don't have to have treatment they don't want and can rely on someone they select to speak for them when they can't. They can refuse additional treatment, opt for hospice care, and hasten their death by refusing food and water. These choices work to give the terminally ill more control, but they still haven't gone far enough.

In a survey of 30,000 Americans over the age of 55, 65% said that people with a terminal illness should have a legal right to hasten their death with a doctor's assistance.

In a survey of 30,000 Americans over the age of 55, 65% said that people with a terminal illness should have a legal right to hasten their death with a doctor's assistance. Carol Poenisch, the adult daughter of a woman with Lou Gehrig's disease who ended her life with the help of Kevorkian, described her mother's condition in the *New England Journal of Medicine*. Her mother could not speak, support her head, or swallow. Extreme weakness meant she required help to do everything. When she discovered that Kevorkian could help her die, she made that choice. According to her daughter, "She was much more at ease with her illness and her death than I. She was much braver about it, and she was calm." Her mother's decision was not unusual for people suffering from this debilitating disorder—56% of patients with Lou Gehrig's disease say they would consider making the same choice.

After three operations for lung cancer, a 62-year-old woman could hardly breathe and suffered suffocating chest pain. Although hospice care helped with her symptoms, she was ready to die. She contacted the Hemlock Society, which provides information and support for a peaceful death. Through the Caring Friends program, a trained volunteer worked with her and her husband to ensure that she had exhausted all the alternatives, that she knew the right way to end her life, and that a medical professional was in attendance when she died. The woman found a compassionate physician who, risking his license and liberty, supplied her with the right amount of lethal medication. She died peacefully, in the company of her husband, best friend, and a Caring Friends volunteer. Because this woman lived in a state where assisting a death is illegal, everyone involved, including the Hemlock Society, could have been subject to prosecution.

The role of doctors

Why is it necessary to involve doctors? Why can't people just kill themselves? In this country, suicide is not a crime. However, suicide, as it traditionally is thought of, involves violence, uncertainty, and pain for the family. Some terminally ill people end their lives while they can, often prematurely, fearing there will be no way to do it if they wait too long. Without the reassurance that someone would be there to help, people often commit suicide violently and use the wrong methods, which can traumatize their loved ones in the process.

Austin Bastable, a Canadian man with multiple sclerosis, who died with the help of Kevorkian, said, "Knowing that such dedicated people exist, I could afford to live longer than I originally had planned—because I knew that I no longer had to rely solely upon my limited abilities to end my life." Those with terminal illnesses should be able to die peacefully, gently, quickly, and with certainty—in the arms of people they love. This requires medical assistance.

Let's consider a typical case, that of Rose, an 82-year-old woman with terminal pancreatic cancer. She has made peace with her dying and receives care at home from a hospice nurse. She is on a morphine pump to control her pain, although she dislikes being sedated. Weak, tired, and nauseated, she knows the end is near and begs for a quick, peaceful death. Her children want to help her, but, because aiding her to die is against the law, they can only watch while she suffers.

Many people, like Rose's children, have cared for a loved one who wants to die, but cannot get the assistance to make it happen. Asking someone for help to die, or being asked to help, is not only emotionally difficult, it could lead to breaking the law.

This tortuous situation occurs every day. If she were hooked up to some kind of treatment, Rose could legally and easily request that it be stopped and she could die, but she isn't. So her children must stand by when their mother is begging them to help her die, and they have to continue to watch her suffer.

Except in Oregon, the law does not allow the family to work with a terminally ill patient's doctor to help end his or her suffering. Some physicians in other states break the law and provide assistance; some family members try to help, but don't know how, and the attempt fails tragically. The patient and the family should be able to discuss their end-of-life choices with their doctor and explore all other alternatives, but be able to know there will be aid in dying if the situation is hopeless and the request persistent.

Patients can make decisions about treatment

Each of us needs to make plans to ensure that the end of life remains in our control. Just as we write wills to dispose of our worldly goods, we can make decisions about what medical treatment is acceptable and what is not. You can write a living will, which says you do not want drastic measures taken if you have no hope for recovery. You can choose a person to make your health care decisions if you are unable to. (This is called the Durable Power of Attorney for Health Care or Health Care Proxy.) That individual should be someone you trust, who knows what you want, and will fight for your rights.

Except in Oregon, the law does not allow the family to work with a terminally ill patient's doctor to help end his or her suffering.

If you agree that physician aid in dying should also be a choice for terminally ill, mentally competent adults who request it, there are things you can do:

• Join an advocacy organization, such as the Hemlock Society, that supports legal change.

• Tell your state and national representatives how you feel.

• Vote if there is an initiative in your state.

• Discuss the issue with your family, doctor, and spiritual advisor.

How you die should be your choice. As poet Archibald MacLeish said, "Freedom is the right to choose: the right to create for yourself the alternative of choice. Without the possibility of choice and the exercise of choice, a man is not a man but a member, an instrument, a thing."

Chronology of right-to-die milestones

1974—First American hospice is founded in Connecticut.

1976—The New Jersey Supreme Court grants the parents of Karen Ann Quinlan permission to remove her from a ventilator after she has been in a coma for a year. She died 10 years later at age 31, having been in a persistent vegetative state, but able to breathe on her own.

1976—The first living will law is passed in California, permitting a person to sign a declaration stating that, if there were no hope of recovery, no heroic measures would be taken to prolong life. Living wills are now available in every state.

1980—The Hemlock Society is formed to advocate for physician-assisted dying for terminally ill, mentally competent adults who request it as one option in the continuum of care.

1983—The first Durable Power of Attorney law is passed in California. It permits an advance directive to be made, describing the kind of health care that would be wanted when facing death and designating a proxy to speak for the person. This provision is now available in every state.

1990—The Supreme Court rules that the parents of Nancy Cruzan, a 32-year-old woman who has been unconscious since a 1983 car accident, cannot remove her feeding tube and let her die. Because this young woman had not completed a living will, no clear and convincing evidence of her wishes existed. When additional evidence of her wishes was later presented, her parents received permission to remove her from life support and she died later that year. The Court did rule, however, that every American could refuse unwanted medical treatment, including food and water, and that each person could appoint a proxy to make health care decisions if he or she could not.

1990—Jack Kevorkian, a retired pathologist, uses his suicide machine to help Janet Adkins, a 54-year-old woman with Alzheimer's disease, end her life at her request.

1991—Congress passes the Patient Self-Determination Act, requiring all Federally funded health care facilities to explain to patients, on admission, that they have the right to complete an advance directive.

1991—Timothy Quill, a primary care physician, publishes an article in the *New England Journal of Medicine* describing how he had prescribed a lethal dose of sedatives to end the life of a young woman whose suffering from leukemia had become unbearable.

1991—Derek Humphry's book, *Final Exit: The Practicalities of Self Deliverance and Assisted Suicide for the Dying*, appears on *The New York Times* best seller list for 18 weeks. It has since been translated into 14 languages.

1994—The people of Oregon vote to legalize physician-assisted dying. State courts delayed passage of the law for three years.

1996—The 2nd and 9th U.S. Circuit Courts of Appeals rule that there is a constitutional right under the 14th Amendment for a terminally ill person to receive help in dying from a doctor.

1996–97—Kevorkian is charged with murder in five cases of physician-assisted suicide and acquitted in each.

1997—The Supreme Court overturns both 1996 circuit court decisions, ruling that it is up to the states to enact laws regarding medically assisted death.

1997—The voters of Oregon reaffirm their support for the Death with Dignity Act by a 60% majority, and the law goes into effect.

1998—Kevorkian administers a lethal injection to Thomas Youk, a 52-year-old man with Lou Gehrig's disease, on national television.

1999—Kevorkian is convicted of second-degree murder for Youk's death and sentenced to 10 to 20 years in prison.

1999—A report in the *New England Journal of Medicine* reveals that 23 terminally ill patients received lethal medication under the Oregon Death with Dignity Act in 1998; 15 took the medication and died peacefully.

1999—Rep. Henry Hyde (R.-Ill.) and Sen. Don Nickles (R.-Okla.) cosponsor the Pain Relief Promotion Act, a bill that would prevent doctors from using Federally regulated drugs to help patients die. The bill, which passed the House of Representatives in October 1999 and reached the Senate in 2000, would override the Oregon law allowing physician-assisted suicide. [The bill did not pass.]

1999—The American Medical Association, at the request of the Oregon Medical Association, allows its House of Delegates to reconsider the AMA's position on the Pain Relief Promotion Act. The AMA House of Delegates decided to continue to back the bill, but withdrew its support of the enforcement provisions in the act.

6

Society Does Not Support the Legalization of Physician-Assisted Suicide

Ezekiel J. Emanuel

Ezekiel J. Emanuel is an oncologist and chief of the department of clinical bioethics at the Clinical Center of the National Institutes of Health.

Public opinion is shifting against physician-assisted suicide. Society does not support the legalization of acts that end the lives of terminally ill patients. Modern medicine has made great advances in the fields of pain management and end-of-life care, making physician-assisted suicide and euthanasia unnecessary. Consequently, proponents of physician-assisted suicide and euthanasia may be part of a dead movement.

Jack Kevorkian's luck has finally run out. After three previous acquittals, the poster boy for euthanasia was convicted of second-degree murder on March 26, 1999, and sentenced to ten to 25 years in prison. "You had the audacity to go on national television, show the world what you did, and dare the prosecution to stop you," Judge Jessica Cooper told Dr. Death. "Well, sir, consider yourself stopped."

Stopping Kevorkian, of course, isn't the same thing as stopping euthanasia and physician-assisted suicide, but his downfall is emblematic of a larger consensus developing against these practices. In the courts, in state legislatures, in public opinion polls, and in the medical community, advocates for euthanasia and assisted suicide are losing the legal and political battle. Indeed, as Americans look more closely at the consequences of euthanasia and assisted suicide—and as physicians develop better ways to care for the dying—it's the argument for these practices that may soon be put out of its misery.

The argument is an old one. In modern times, it was first articulated by Samuel Williams, in an 1870 speech before the Birmingham (England) Speculative Club. "In all cases of hopeless and painful illness," he said, "it should be the recognized duty of the medical attendant, whenever so desired by the patient, to administer chloroform . . . so as to destroy consciousness at once, and put the sufferer to a quick and painless death." Williams's speech caused a political and medical uproar in Great Britain, and, before long, the debate had landed on American shores. In 1905, "An Act Concerning Administration of Drugs, etc. to Mortally Injured and Diseased Persons"—a bill to legalize euthanasia—was introduced in the Ohio legislature and hotly discussed across the country.

Ultimately, though, the legislature rejected the bill 79 to 23. Interest among Americans gradually waned—the issue becoming, in the words of the *Journal of American Medicine*, "like a recurring decimal." It wasn't until about ten years ago, thanks to Kevorkian's antics and, more substantively, to a pair of articles in the *Journal of the American Medical Association* and the *New England Journal of Medicine*, that the issue resurfaced nationally. Initial legalization attempts were for both euthanasia and physician-assisted suicide. More recent efforts have been geared primarily toward legalizing assisted suicide, although in practice the distinction is dubious.

The tide began to shift against the assisted-suicide movement in 1997, when the Supreme Court unanimously ruled against a constitutional right to assisted suicide or euthanasia; Florida's Supreme Court did the same thing weeks later. At the level of state politics, 70 percent of Michigan voters opposed a 1998 referendum to legalize assisted suicide. Although many states have considered bills to legalize euthanasia or physician-assisted suicide, few bills have made it out of committee, and none has passed a legislative body. Moreover, since the U.S. Supreme Court ruling, three states have passed laws specifically criminalizing physician-assisted suicide, thus joining the 35 states that already had such statutes.

While conventional wisdom holds that most Americans support the legalization of euthanasia and physician-assisted suicide, slight changes in wording and emphasis can elicit contradictory responses. For instance, while a majority of adults may favor allowing doctors "by law to assist the patient to commit suicide if the patient requests it," less than half agree with the idea that "it should be legal for a doctor to help a terminally ill patient commit suicide." Patients and their families have begun to realize that there may be more to a "good death" than speed and physical comfort. People often need time to say good-bye to family and friends, take care of practical things, or attend to spiritual matters. Also, key segments of the population—the elderly, the religious, African Americans, and women—are strongly opposed to legalization.

Support of the medical profession is in decline

Support for euthanasia and assisted suicide has declined rapidly among those who must administer it. In 1994, a research group I headed conducted a poll among oncologists and found that 46 percent supported physician-assisted suicide for a terminally ill cancer patient with unremitting pain; 23 percent supported euthanasia. A repeat national survey of oncologists I headed in 1998 showed that support for physician-assisted suicide in the same circumstance had declined by half, to 22 percent; support for euthanasia had declined even more, to a mere six percent of cancer doctors.

Increasingly, the medical profession is looking for ways to improve care for the dying rather than accede to assisted suicide. The Institute of Medicine released a major study on dying in America with numerous recommendations on how it could be improved, and the National Institutes of Health has designated millions of dollars for research on improvements. The American Medical Association has developed a comprehensive curriculum—Education for Physicians on End-of-Life Care—on caring for dying patients. Similarly, medical schools are beginning to enhance their teaching of pain management and end-of-life care.

In the courts, in state legislatures, in public opinion polls, and in the medical community, advocates for euthanasia and assisted suicide are losing the legal and political battle.

Another force behind the shift may be the movement itself, or at least elements of it. Kevorkian's made-for-TV euthanasia of Thomas Youk highlighted some of the major arguments against euthanasia—namely, that euthanasia may be used as a replacement for palliative care rather than as a "last ditch" treatment and that patients may be pressured into ending their lives. Youk, who suffered from Lou Gehrig's disease, was experiencing no pain but worried about caring for himself and burdening his family. Kevorkian did absolutely nothing to be sure that Youk received appropriate alternatives—like home care or a psychiatric evaluation—before he went for the lethal needle. Then there was the fact that, when Youk evinced some hesitation about going ahead with the injection, the video was interrupted. While we do not know what Kevorkian or Youk's family said to him during the interruption, the video left the impression that Youk may have been pressured into his decision.

The results of the assisted-suicide movement's greatest victory to date—a 1994 referendum victory that legalized physician-assisted suicide in Oregon—have not helped, either. Only 15 patients (13 of whom had cancer) ended their lives by assisted suicide in the first 14 months under the new law, which took effect in 1997. A study found that, in general, these patients were not experiencing excruciating pain. Indeed, only one of the patients complained of inadequate pain control. This confirmed other studies that show that pain is not the main—and not even an important—factor in motivating patients to request euthanasia or assisted suicide; plainly, the conventional notion of why a terminally ill person would want to end his life is simply false.

Physician-assisted suicide has cost appeal

The Oregon data casts further doubt on the need for legalization at all. In 1998, 28,913 Oregonians died. Fifteen patients represent a miniscule 0.05 percent of all dying patients in Oregon. By contrast, in the Netherlands, more than three percent of patients die by euthanasia or physician-assisted suicide. Either there is very little demand and hence little need for legalized physician-assisted suicide in the United States or there is a lot of euthanasia and physician-assisted suicide going on outside the law, undermining the notion that legalization is the only way to ensure regulation and enforcement of safeguards.

As the history from the Gilded Age suggests, public enthusiasm for assisted suicide and euthanasia seems to flourish at times of economic instability and when the reigning social philosophy is laissez-faire. Interest in euthanasia waned with the rise of the Progressive movement and as trust in government and professionals increased. Interestingly, the recent resurgence of public interest in euthanasia coincided with the economic uncertainty of the early '90s and the high tide of Republican free-market ideology. But this ethos is no longer as salient as it used to be, particularly when it comes to health care. With the rise of managed care, government and physicians now seem to be the public's allies and protectors. In such an atmosphere, euthanasia and physician-assisted suicide no longer seem so appealing.

Proponents will continue to press legal cases, to lobby legislatures, and to try to get on the ballot. But these efforts will be largely irrelevant. The clamor for euthanasia and physician-assisted suicide pushed medical professionals to improve end-of-life care. With those changes established, the assisted-suicide movement itself may be in terminal condition.

7

Legalizing Physician-Assisted Suicide Would Lead to Patient Abuse

Kevin Irvine

Kevin Irvine is a member of Not Dead Yet, a disability-rights action group that works to prevent the legalization of physician-assisted suicide.

The U.S. health care system takes a bottom-line approach to medical care and views disabled and terminally-ill patients as expenses. As a result, if health care providers were given legal authority to carry out physician-assisted suicide, they would do so even against patients' wishes because such an approach would reduce the costs of caring for the seriously ill.

People with AIDS tend to have a skewed view of legalizing physician-assisted suicide. We usually think about it only in terms of our own illness. We remember those who died from painful, debilitating diseases and infections, and this understandably makes some of us want a degree of control over the end of life. Living with both severe hemophilia and HIV, I had a similar view until I became an activist in the larger disability community. Since then I've come to believe that legalizing assisted suicide will have a devastating effect on how people with other, nonterminal disabilities, such as multiple sclerosis, cerebral palsy and muscular dystrophy, are treated by the health care system.

Quality of life means one thing for someone who is 42 and has been battling full-blown AIDS for five years, and something entirely different for a 22-year-old with a spinal-cord injury who may live 60 more years. Making assisted suicide legal will let the PWA [Person with AIDS] decide when enough is enough, but it will likely encourage the youth—who now, unable to afford the personal assistance needed to live independently at home, is forced into a nursing home, who cannot get a job because of discrimination and who is viewed as an object of pity—in the belief that life is not worth living. Instead of fighting to make it easier for this 22-year-old to die, I think we should fight to make his or her life better—with adequate health care, home and community services, jobs, public transit, benefits—and role models who've successfully dealt with the same disability.

Not Dead Yet, a disability-rights action group, is deeply concerned about the dangers of legalizing assisted suicide. For over two years, the group has brought a different, previously unheard perspective to this debate. In doing so, we've found ourselves allied with some strange bedfellows, such as the American Medical Association (AMA) and "right to life" groups; unlike most of them, however, our motivation comes not from a religious belief in the sanctity of life but from someplace deeper: Fear. We fear that the discrimination faced every day by people with disabilities will lead to widespread abuse of assisted suicide. Many people—including our friends, family members and doctors—still think (and say out loud) that it would be better to be dead than disabled.

Physician-assisted death [is] the ultimate money-saver [for hospitals]. That thought scares me to my core.

Since Bill Clinton's administration abandoned the drive for a universal health care system four years ago in 1994, mangled care has grown like a cancer. My own Health Maintenance Organization (HMO), owned by Cigna Corp., proposed a system to give cash rewards to doctors whose patients cost less and have fewer procedures. This bottom-line approach to medicine wrests control from physicians and consumers and cedes it to the bean counters. These are the values of the system into which we plan to introduce physician-assisted death, the ultimate money-saver. That thought scares me to my core.

Inadequate end-of-life care

My fears have taken root from seeds already planted in our current arrangements for dying. Patients entering hospitals, especially those with disabilities, are repeatedly urged to sign DNRs (Do Not Resuscitate orders, which allow the hospital to unilaterally avoid extensive life-preserving measures regardless of the emergency), even when under the influence of narcotic medication or severe stress. Some hospitals have policies prohibiting life-saving procedures for people with certain disabilities. Many people—having never unlearned society's scorn of what life with a disability is like—prepare living wills prior to any hospitalization. One woman who signed such a document had a stroke, wound up in the hospital partially paralyzed and decided she wanted to live. But the hospital refused her pleas for food and water, and she starved to death 10 days later.

Most doctors admit to having inadequate training in treating people with chronic disabilities and end-stage illness, especially in the proper management of pain and depression, which would lessen, if not prevent, much suffering. While some people with full-blown AIDS will not "get better," others with nonterminal disabilities will have symptoms and life situations that wax and wane. One man with multiple sclerosis said he was seeking the so-called [euthanasia] services of Dr. Jack Kevorkian to avoid having to go into "a rat-infested nursing home."

People get better

If assisted suicide were legal, for every person who will make a careful, reasoned decision to end his or her life, there will likely be those who act in haste, under pressure, when they feel their life is meaningless and a burden to others. And for those who view their doctor as close to a god and faithfully follow every treatment regimen, how powerful to hear a physician offering the possibility of a relatively painless death as a "solution"— a permanent one. It's worth recalling the grim climate in the AIDS community in 1995, before the widespread use of protease combinations [drugs]. Now, as I write this, the Centers for Disease Control (CDC) has just announced that AIDS is no longer the No. 1 killer of adults aged 25 to 44. We all know people facing a death sentence who've staged remarkable recoveries. Had physician-assisted death been legal back when hope was scarce, some wouldn't be around today.

At a time when the fight against AIDS holds more promise than ever and yet our dreams of equality and justice are deferred, why do we waste energy fighting to grant our mangled medical system more power to get rid of us? To think we can control this genie once it's out of the bottle flies in the face of all the evidence. I don't trust our society to handle assisted suicide any better than it has handled the AIDS epidemic. I plead with my community to move beyond its skewed view and listen to *all* of the people who will be affected by physician-assisted suicide.

8

Legalizing Physician-Assisted Suicide Would Not Lead to Patient Abuse

Dan W. Brock

Dan W. Brock is a professor of philosophy and biomedical ethics at Brown University and director of Brown's Center for Biomedical Ethics.

Concerns that the legalization of physician-assisted suicide (PAS) would lead to patient abuse are unfounded. Laws regulating PAS would include important safeguards that would protect dying patients. Opponents of PAS fear that many patients would choose physician-assisted suicide because they do not have access to quality end-of-life care, but denying them the option of a speedy death would be an additional cruelty. Although many critics worry that more patients will be coerced into choosing PAS because it is cheaper than providing end-of-life care, there is no evidence that PAS would actually be cheaper nor that people would choose it over other options. Finally, legalization of PAS would not result in non–terminally ill patients choosing it because the laws regulating the practice would limit it to the dying.

C onsider . . . the fundamental, though rarely articulated, assumption underlying the potential-for-abuse objection to physician-assisted suicide (PAS). That assumption is that the practices with limited potential for abuse are the forgoing of life support, pain relief that hastens death, and, perhaps, terminal sedation; whether the decisions are made by competent patients or the surrogates of incompetent patients; whereas the potential for abuse is much greater with PAS and even greater with voluntary active euthanasia (VAE). . . . Determining which cases to count as abuses is itself controversial, but the importance widely accorded to informed consent and advance directives, at least in the case of forgoing life support, pain relief that hastens death, and terminal sedation, suggests wide agreement that decisions should follow the patient's wishes; decisions which conflict with what patients do or would want are abuses. The same standard is implicit in the potential abuses typically cited by opponents of PAS, which are subtle or unsubtle pressures for PAS that the patient does not or would not want. If this is roughly the correct standard for what constitutes abuses, then even in the absence of data there is strong reason to believe that the common assumption about which practices are most subject to abuse is mistaken. Instead, the important distinction for the potential for abuse is between those practices in which the competent patient makes the decision for him- or herself and other practices in which the patient is incompetent and someone else must decide for the patient. A number of studies have documented that neither physicians nor family members can reliably predict patients' preferences regarding end-of-life care in the absence of explicit and specific discussion with the patient.[1] Even when surrogate decision makers attempt only to determine what the patient would have wanted, they will often fail to do so correctly. Moreover, when surrogate decision makers have conflicts between their own interests or desires, or the interests or desires of others about whom they care, and those of the patient, we can expect further conflicts between their decisions and what the patients for whom they are acting would have wanted. This supports a strong presumption that the point at which the potential for abuse increases substantially in end-of-life care decisions is when surrogate decision makers must decide for incompetent patients instead of competent patients deciding for themselves. And, of course, this means, in turn, that PAS (and even VAE) are among the end-of-life decisions and practices less subject to abuse than are decisions by surrogates for incompetent patients to forgo life support, use pain relief that may hasten death, or employ terminal sedation. But are there other reasons for thinking that, despite this presumption, overall, PAS would be more subject to abuse than these other widely accepted practices of surrogate decision making in end-of-life care?

Important safeguards

One very important factor affecting the potential for abuse of any practice is what safeguards are erected to guard against the abuses most feared and likely. Proposals for model legislation to permit PAS, as well as the proposal [the Death with Dignity Act] that was adopted by referendum in the state of Oregon in 1997, typically have substantial safeguards.[2] They include that the patient be:

an adult;

diagnosed to be terminally ill (i.e., likely to die within six months, even with treatment);

suffering from an unbearable and irreversible physical illness or condition;

informed about his or her diagnosis, prognosis without treatment, possible treatment alternatives that might improve that prognosis, along with their risks and benefits (typically with a required evaluation of the patient by a second physician to confirm the diagnosis and prognosis, and documentation and witnessing of the discussion with the patient);

offered other available alternatives, in particular, hospice care and other palliative services that might improve the patient's condition and change the desire for PAS;

evaluated for competence by a qualified mental health professional, in particular, to ensure that the patient's decision for PAS is not the result of treatable clinical depression;

making an enduring (e.g., with a waiting period of one or two weeks from the first request until the means for PAS are made available to the patient) and voluntary (free from undue influence) request for PAS;

reported to regulatory authorities, in a manner that protects patient confidentiality while permitting oversight of the practice, as having requested and received PAS.

Safeguards like these would not eliminate all potential for abuse of PAS—no set of safeguards could do that, and no practices in the real world are guaranteed to be free of all possible abuse. But the status quo (in which PAS is generally illegal) is not free of abuse either. One abuse of current public policy is that in all the states, except Oregon, that prohibit PAS, PAS still occurs, but not openly and without any safeguards, such as those above, to control its practice. And if we compare the practices of forgoing life support, using pain medications that may hasten death, and terminal sedation, whether decisions are made by a competent patient or by a surrogate for an incompetent patient—in no state are any of the formal safeguards listed above in use, although all of these other practices, like PAS, also result in the death of the patient. This is further reason to believe that PAS would be less, not more, subject to abuse than these other widely accepted practices. Opponents of PAS, nevertheless, often point to the Netherlands, where there are a significant number of cases [of physician-assisted suicide] in which somewhat less restrictive safeguards are not fully adhered to, as evidence that these safeguards would be ineffective in the United States.[3] The opponents are correct in stating that the safeguards would not be fully effective, but it is difficult to see why they would not at least reduce the potential for abuse with PAS to a level below current levels for other practices that also result in death but lack any comparable safeguards.

Opponents also argue that the potential for abuse would be greater with PAS than with forgoing life support and pain relief that may hasten death because many more people would be at risk of receiving PAS since it would not be restricted to patients receiving some form of life support. But this is mistaken for at least two reasons. First, if PAS is restricted to the terminally ill, as it is in Oregon and in most of the proposals to legalize it, this would substantially limit those eligible for it and limit as well the amount of life that would be lost by any patient who did it; by contrast, patients can and do refuse life-sustaining treatment who are not terminally ill and who sometimes give up many years of possible life. It is difficult to know whether the potential pool of persons eligible for PAS would be larger or smaller than the pool of patients eligible to refuse life support. Second, and more important, we do know that in the Netherlands, where PAS and VAE have been permitted for more than a decade, many times the number of patients die from withholding or withdrawing life-sustaining treatment and pain relief that hastens death than from PAS and VAE. In the 1995 update of the original Remmelink study of 1990, it was estimated that 2.6 percent of all deaths were the result of PAS and VAE (and another 0.7 percent were from ending life without the patient's explicit request at the time at which life was ended), but 20.2 percent were from a decision to forgo treatment and another 19.1 percent were from the use of opioids in large doses.[4]

Concerns about health care

Are there, nevertheless, features of PAS that would make it more likely to be abused than decisions to forgo treatment or pain relief that hastens death? Opponents of PAS who focus on the potential for abuse typically cite several possible illegitimate motivations and incentives for PAS. First, with over 40 million Americans now without health insurance, many persons might choose PAS only because they cannot obtain adequate health care at the end of life. Second, even for patients with health insurance, there are well-documented and widespread inadequacies in end-of-life care that could lead patients to choose PAS who would not do so if they had access to higher quality end-of-life care; the widespread failure to provide dying patients with adequate pain management and control is a special concern.[5] Moreover, the availability of the "easier out" of PAS might undermine society's and physicians' motivations to improve the care of dying patients. Third, dying patients are often difficult and demanding to care for, are seen as the failures of medicine by many health-care professionals, and are emotionally draining on family members. Moreover, many dying patients are frail, frightened, vulnerable, and in a poor position to assert their needs and interests. If PAS is legalized, these factors could combine to lead to subtle manipulation or pressuring of some patients to choose PAS who would not really want it. Fourth, in an era of rapid growth of managed care in which cost containment dominates the health-policy agenda, PAS may be seen as a money-saving alternative to very expensive care of critically ill and dying patients, further pressuring such patients to choose PAS. Each of these concerns makes empirical claims for which data are scanty at best, yet the scope and probability of the feared effects are crucial to the weight they should be accorded; empirical research is at least as important as philosophical analysis in responding to them. Nevertheless, we can at least consider briefly whether they are more serious concerns about PAS than about forgoing of life support and pain relief that may hasten death.

The first two concerns, that patients without, and even with, health insurance will only seek PAS because they cannot obtain adequate end-of-life health care, are related. The safeguards proposed for PAS will provide some assurance that patients are informed about treatment and other alternatives, such as hospice care, but they will not always assure that those alternatives will be available and affordable. Some commentators have argued that the threat of PAS being permitted will lead, or already is leading, to strengthened efforts to improve end-of-life care, so as to reduce the pressure to permit PAS and to ensure that if it is permitted, few patients will choose it. However, we do know that even if PAS is permitted only a very small proportion of dying patients will choose it; consequently, we will still have to care for the vast majority of dying patients who do not choose it. All the reasons and motivations for professional and public concern to improve the care of dying patients, which have generated a host of important initiatives now underway, will remain in place. But there undoubtedly would be some patients who choose PAS who would not do so if better end-of-life care were available to them, just as there are now patients who forgo life support who would not do so if better end-of-life care were available to them. This is clearly a strong reason to improve the care of such patients, but is it also a strong reason to oppose permitting PAS, as many opponents suppose? I believe it is not.

Our failure to provide high quality end-of-life care for all dying patients creates a cruel dilemma for public policy which should be recognized and acknowledged for what it is. Even if the many efforts now under way to improve the care of dying patients all prove immensely successful, there are two kinds of patients who will still prefer PAS. The first are patients who, even with optimal end-of-life care, will still prefer PAS because it best fits their view of a humane and dignified death; for these patients PAS is genuinely the best alternative mode of dying, and they constitute no policy reason for opposing PAS. The second kind of patient would not prefer PAS if they could get better end-of-life care, but since they cannot, they want PAS. What is the cruel dilemma that these patients pose for public policy? On the one hand, policy makers' or individual physicians' reluctance to provide these patients with PAS is quite understandable, knowing that they would not want it if they could get better end-of-life care. On the other hand, we should be equally reluctant to deny them the PAS they want and to make them endure a dying process they find worse than an earlier death by PAS, on the grounds that they would not want PAS if they could get better end-of-life care. To those patients, the prohibition of PAS in effect says this: "You cannot have the PAS that, in your circumstances, you quite reasonably want, but instead must endure a dying process that you find worse than an earlier death by PAS. Why? Because you would not want PAS if your care was further improved, although it will not be." To those patients, that is indeed a cruel death sentence. The resolution of this dilemma is not simply to prohibit PAS, but both to galvanize efforts to improve the care of all dying patients and to make PAS available to those patients for whom PAS remains preferable to the best care available to them.

Physician-assisted suicide would be less, not more, subject to abuse than . . . other widely accepted practices [that hasten death].

So the response to the first two concerns about abuse of PAS based on limits in access to health care generally, or to adequate end-of-life care in particular, is, first, that these may as easily lead patients to forgo life support when they would not if better end-of-life care were available and, second, that this concern regarding PAS does not support prohibiting it but, rather, both improving end-of-life care together with permitting PAS for those patients for whom it remains the better and preferred alternative.

The third and fourth concerns above are also related—they focus on the medical, emotional, and financial burdensomeness of critically ill and dying patients to their caretakers, families, and insurance plans, and the incentives these others may consequently have subtly, or even overtly, to manipulate or pressure them to accept PAS. Part of the answer to this concern lies in the safeguards noted above that are designed to ensure that requests for PAS are made without undue influence or pressure from others. Since these go well beyond any current safeguards for decisions to forgo treatment, it is hard to see why the burdens created by dying patients should not, if anything, more easily and frequently lead to undue influence or pressure on patients or surrogates of incompetent patients to forgo treatment than to choose PAS. And yet there are no data to my knowledge to support that involuntary choices to forgo life support are at all common, although they no doubt do sometimes occur. There is little anecdotal evidence, much less any well-documented problem, of frail, fearful, and vulnerable patients now being pressured to accept earlier deaths than they wish, nor is there good reason to believe that this would occur with PAS if it were permitted.

Finally, the financial concern that PAS would be a cost-saving alternative to high-quality care of dying patients is not well founded. A recent paper, coauthored by a strong opponent and a strong proponent of PAS, estimates the potential cost savings possible from the introduction of PAS and concludes that the savings would be negligible and insufficient to create strong incentives, within managed care plans, for example, to pressure patients to accept PAS.[6]

The slippery-slope worry

There is one last aspect of the fear-of-abuse objection to PAS that I want to pursue briefly. This is a specifically slippery-slope worry that, although PAS would initially be restricted, for example, to competent terminally ill adults with safeguards like those noted above, the practice would soon be expanded and loosened beyond control, to VAE as well as PAS, and to patients who are not terminally ill, to children and the mentally ill, to incompetent patients, either on the basis of their advance directives or of surrogates choosing for them, and ending, finally, with persons for whom there is no longer any pretense that PAS or VAE serve their wishes, imitating the Nazi euthanasia program to rid society of "useless eaters and burdens." Slippery-slope worries of this sort represent different kinds of worries about abuse than those I have been considering above because they do not claim the specific practices of PAS being proposed would be seriously abused. Instead, they are commonly grounded in two sorts of claims: first, that the logic of the arguments offered in support of the restricted practice of PAS now proposed extends as well, and so would be applied over time, to a much broader practice of killing; second, that introducing even a restricted practice of PAS would erode over time society's respect for human life so that we would come to tolerate or accept an ever-expanding practice of killing.

Consider the first sort of claim, that the logic of the arguments of supporters of PAS extends, for example, to nonterminally ill and incompetent patients, and to VAE as well as PAS. Moreover, opponents of PAS point out, in the case of rights of competent terminally ill patients to refuse life support, those rights have in fact been extended in this way to nonterminally ill patients and to decisions based on advance directives or made by surrogates for incompetent patients, in each case in important part because the logic of the initial arguments did apply more broadly. I noted in the introduction to the article that had the Supreme Court upheld a constitutional right of terminally ill patients to PAS, that right might well have been vulnerable to challenges seeking to extend it in exactly these ways. But left as public policy decisions for the states to determine to whom and when, if at all, to make PAS available, states are free to make their own reasonable assessments of the benefits and risks of various extensions of PAS to broader classes of persons and/or to VAE. Nevertheless, it is correct in my view that the fundamental moral principles and values that justify a restricted practice of PAS for competent, terminally ill adults do apply more broadly, though not so far as some opponents claim, and it is either a mistake or dishonest for supporters of PAS to deny that in the hopes of avoiding the broader controversies.

Many times the number of patients die from withholding or withdrawing life-sustaining treatment and pain relief that hastens death than from physician-assisted suicide.

But it need be neither a mistake nor dishonest to limit the argument now, as I have done here, to the more restricted practice. Initially permitting only the more restricted practice would be quite reasonable social policy in order to gain evidence about the degree to which it can be adequately safeguarded and controlled. That evidence would be of fundamental importance in making any later policy judgments about the wisdom of extending the practice more broadly. There is a moral cost in restricting a practice of PAS to competent and terminally ill patients and to permitting only PAS and not VAE. There are equally compelling moral reasons for some nonterminally ill patients undergoing intolerable suffering, for some patients who have lost the capacity to make their own decisions but who clearly would have wanted actively to end their lives, and for some patients unable to perform the last physical action of ending of their own lives, all to have access to a broader practice of PAS and to VAE. The restricted practice of PAS that I have been concerned with in this section of the paper would deny PAS and/or VAE to some persons when, considering only the individual cases, there are compelling moral reasons to permit PAS and/or VAE. But if PAS is extended to non–terminally ill patients, the seriousness and costs of abuses or mistakes increase, and if VAE is permitted for incompetent patients based on their advance directives or on their surrogates' decisions, the risks of decisions that do not reflect the true wishes of the patient increase substantially. The potential risks of increased seriousness and frequency of abuse from these extensions or expansions of PAS may or may not be too great to warrant doing so. But even if the logic of the argument for the restricted practice of PAS does extend more broadly, it is not unreasonable caution to wait until we have experience with the more restricted practice before we decide which, if any, additional steps we wish to take on the slope.

The other version of the slippery slope worry is that any practice of actively taking life, such as PAS, will inevitably erode respect for human life and set us on a path toward ever wider killing. Only time and experience with a practice of PAS could decisively refute this concern, but the fundamental role of individual self-determination or autonomy in the broad social movement over the last several decades in the United States to secure for patients control over their dying, a movement driven principally by patients and potential patients—that is, the public—is a formidable bulwark against heading down that feared path. Respecting the self-determination of individual human beings in no way supports practices that would take the lives of persons against their wishes or because doing so might serve the interests of others.

As I stated at the outset of this section, there is no denying the presence of widespread concern that PAS would be subject to much greater abuse than are the currently accepted practices of forgoing life support, pain relief that can hasten death, and terminal sedation. I have suggested a number of reasons, however, why I believe that concern is not well founded. Indeed, I would reiterate that abuse and mistake are more likely in practices in which surrogates make decisions for incompetent patients; concern to prevent abuse by erecting safeguards to protect patients might better focus there than on PAS.

Notes

1. Richard F. Uhlmann, Robert A. Pearlman, and K.C. Cain, "Physicians' and Spouses' Predictions of Elderly Patients' Treatment Preferences," *Journal of Gerontology* 43 (1988): 115–21; Tom Tomlinson et al., "An Empirical Study of Proxy Consent for Elderly Persons," *Gerontologist* 30 (1990): 54–61; Robert A. Pearlman, Richard F. Uhlmann, and Nancy S. Jecker, "Spousal Understanding of Patient Quality of Life: Implications for Surrogate Decisions," *Journal of Clinical Ethics* 3 (1992): 114–21.

2. Charles H. Baron, Clyde Bergstrasser, Dan W. Brock et al., "A Model State Statute to Authorize and Regulate Physician-Assisted Suicide," *Harvard Journal of Legislation* 331 (1996): 1–34.

3. Daniel Callahan and Margot White, "The Legalization of Physician-Assisted Suicide: Creating a Regulatory Potemkin Village," *University of Richmond Law Review* 30 (1996): 1–83.

4. Paul F. VanDerMaas, Gerrit VanDerWal, Ilinka Haverkate et al., "Euthanasia, Physician-Assisted Suicide, and Other Medical Practices Involving the End of Life in the Netherlands, 1990–95," *New England Journal of Medicine* 335 (1996): 1699–1705.

5. The SUPPORT Principal Investigators for the SUPPORT Project, "A Controlled Trial to Improve Care for Seriously Ill Hospitalized Patients: The Study to Understand Prognoses and Preferences for Outcomes and Risks of Treatment," *Journal of the American Medical Association* 274 (1995): 1591–98.

6. Ezekiel J. Emanuel and Margaret Battin, "What Are the Potential Cost Savings from Legalizing Physician-Assisted Suicide?" *New England Journal of Medicine* 339 (1998): 167–72.

Organizations to Contact

The editors have compiled the following list of organizations concerned with the issues debated in this book. The descriptions are derived from materials provided by the organizations. All have publications or information available for interested readers. The list was compiled on the date of publication of the present volume; the information provided here may change. Be aware that many organizations take several weeks or longer to respond to inquiries, so allow as much time as possible.

American Civil Liberties Union (ACLU)
125 Broad St., 18th Floor, New York, NY 10004
(212) 549-2500
website: www.aclu.org

The ACLU is a national organization that works to defend civil rights as guaranteed in the U.S. Constitution. It champions the rights of individuals in right-to-die and euthanasia cases as well as cases involving other civil rights issues. The Foundation of the ACLU provides legal defense, research, and education. The organization publishes the quarterly *Civil Liberties* and various pamphlets, books, and position papers.

American Foundation for Suicide Prevention (AFSP)
120 Wall St., 22nd Floor, New York, NY 10005
(888) 333-2377 • fax: (212) 363-6237
e-mail: inquiry@afsp.org • website: www.afsp.org

Formerly known as the American Suicide Foundation, the AFSP supports scientific research on depression and suicide, educates the public and professionals on the recognition and treatment of depressed and suicidal individuals, and provides support programs for those coping with the loss of a loved one to suicide. It opposes the legalization of physician-assisted suicide. AFSP publishes a policy statement on physician-assisted suicide, the newsletter *Crisis*, and the quarterly *Lifesavers*.

American Life League
PO Box 1350, Stafford, VA 22555
(540) 659-4171
e-mail: sysop@all.org • website: www.all.org

The league believes that human life is sacred. It works to educate Americans on the dangers of all forms of euthanasia and opposes legislative efforts that would legalize or increase its incidence. It publishes the bimonthly pro-life magazine *Celebrate Life*; videos; brochures, including "Euthanasia and You" and "Jack Kevorkian: Agent of Death"; and newsletters monitoring abortion- and euthanasia-related legal developments.

American Society of Law, Medicine, and Ethics (ASLME)
765 Commonwealth Ave., Suite 1634, Boston, MA 02215
(617) 262-4990 • fax: (617) 437-7596
e-mail: aslme@bu.edu • website: www.aslme.org

ASLME works to provide scholarship, debate, and critical thought to professionals concerned with legal, health care, policy, and ethical issues. It publishes the *Journal of Law, Medicine, and Ethics* as well as a quarterly newsletter.

Compassion in Dying (CID)
6312 SW Capital Hwy., Suite 415, Portland, OR 97201
(503) 221-9556 • fax: (503) 228-9160
e-mail: info@compassionindying.org • website: www.compassionindying.org

CID believes that dying patients should receive information about all options at the end of life, including those that may hasten death. It provides information on intensive pain management, comfort or hospice care, and humane, effective aid in dying. CID advocates laws that would make assistance in dying legally available for terminally ill, mentally competent adults, and it publishes a newsletter detailing these efforts.

Death with Dignity
11 Dupont Circle NW, Suite 202, Washington, DC 20036
(202) 969-1669 • fax: (202) 969-1668
e-mail: info@deathwithdignity.org • website: www.deathwithdignity.org

Death with Dignity promotes a comprehensive, humane, responsive system of care for terminally ill patients. Its members believe that a dying patient's choices should be given the utmost respect and consideration. The center serves as an information resource for the public and the media and promotes strategies for advancing a responsive system of care for terminally ill patients on educational, legal, legislative, and public-policy fronts. It publishes several fact sheets, including "Misconceptions in the Debate on Death with Dignity," "Dying in the U.S.A.: A Call for Public Debate," and "The Issue: From the Individual's Perspective," all of which are available in an information package by request.

Dying with Dignity
55 Eglinton Ave. East, Suite 705, Toronto, ON M4P 1G8 Canada
(800) 495-6156 • (416) 486-3998 • fax: (416) 489-9010
e-mail: dwdca@web.net • website: www.web.net/dwd

Dying with Dignity works to improve the quality of dying for all Canadians in accordance with their wishes, values, and beliefs. It educates Canadians about their right to choose health care options at the end of life, provides counseling and advocacy services to those who request them, and builds public support for voluntary physician-assisted dying. Dying with Dignity publishes a newsletter and maintains an extensive library of euthanasia-related materials that students may borrow.

Euthanasia Research and Guidance Organization (ERGO)
24829 Norris Ln., Junction City, OR 97448-9559
(541) 998-1873
websites: www.finalexit.org • www.rights.org/~deathnet/ergo.html

ERGO provides information and research findings on physician-assisted dying to persons who are terminally ill and wish to end their suffering. Its members counsel dying patients and develop ethical, psychological, and legal guidelines to help them and their physicians make life-ending decisions. The organization's publications include *Deciding to Die: What You Should Consider* and *Assisting a Patient to Die: A Guide for Physicians.*

The Hemlock Society
PO Box 101810, Denver, CO 80250
(800) 247-7421 • (303) 639-1202 • fax: (303) 639-1224
e-mail: hemlock@hemlock.org • website: www.hemlock.org

The society believes that terminally ill individuals have the right to commit suicide. The society publishes books on suicide, death, and dying, including *Final Exit*, a guide for those suffering with terminal illnesses and considering suicide. The Hemlock Society also publishes the newsletter *TimeLines*.

Human Life International (HLI)
4 Family Life Ln., Front Royal, VA 22630
(540) 635-7884 • fax: (540) 635-7363
e-mail: hli@hli.org • website: www.hli.org

HLI categorically rejects abortion and euthanasia and believes assisted suicide is morally unacceptable. It defends the rights of the unborn, the disabled, and those threatened by euthanasia, and it provides education, advocacy, and support services. HLI publishes the monthly newsletter *HLI Reports*, *HLI Update*, and *Deacons Circle*.

International Anti-Euthanasia Task Force (IAETF)
PO Box 760, Steubenville, OH 43952
(740) 282-3810
e-mail: info@iaetf.org • website: www.iaetf.org

The task force opposes euthanasia, assisted suicide, and policies that threaten the lives of the medically vulnerable. IAETF publishes fact sheets and position papers on euthanasia-related topics in addition to the bimonthly newsletter *IAETF Update*. It analyzes the policies and legislation concerning medical and social work organizations and files amicus curiae briefs in major right-to-die causes.

National Right to Life Committee (NRLC)
419 Seventh St. NW, Suite 500, Washington, DC 20004
(202) 626-8800
e-mail: nrlc@nrlc.org • website: www.NCLR.org

The committee is an activist group that opposes euthanasia and assisted suicide. NRLC publishes the monthly *NRL News* and the four-part position paper "Why We Shouldn't Legalize Assisting Suicide."

Partnership For Caring, Inc.
1620 Eye St. NW, Suite 202, Washington, DC 20006
(202) 296-8071 • fax: (202) 296-8352
e-mail: pfc@partnershipforcaring.org • website: www.partnershipforcaring.org

Partnership For Caring: America's Voices for the Dying is a national nonprofit organization that partners individuals and organizations in a collaboration to improve the manner in which people die. Among other services, Partnership For Caring operates the only national crisis and informational hotline dealing with end-of-life issues and provides state-specific living wills and medical powers of attorney. It publishes fact sheets and articles on end-of-life treatment as well as the newsletter *Voices*.

Bibliography

Books

Gerald Dworkin, R.G. Frey, and Sissela Bok
Euthanasia and Physician-Assisted Suicide: For and Against. New York: Cambridge University Press, 1998.

Peter G. Filene
In the Arms of Others: A Cultural History of the Right to Die in America. Chicago: Ivan R. Dee, 1998.

Elaine Fox et al.
Come Lovely and Soothing Death: The Right to Die Movement in the United States. Farmington Hills, MI: Gale, 1999.

H. Leon Green
If I Should Wake Before I Die: The Medical and Biblical Truth About Near-Death Experiences. Wheaton, IL: Crossway, 1997.

Herbert Hendin
Seduced by Death: Doctors, Patients, and Assisted Suicide. New York: W.W. Norton, 1998.

Derek Humphry and Mary Clement
Freedom to Die: People, Politics, and the Right-to-Die Movement. New York: St. Martin's, 1998.

Edward J. Larson and Darrel W. Amundsen
A Different Death: Euthanasia and the Christian Tradition. Westmont, IL: InterVarsity, 1998.

Marcia Lattanzi-Licht et al.
The Hospice Choice: In Pursuit of a Peaceful Death. New York: Simon & Schuster, 1998.

C.G. Prado and S.J. Taylor
Assisted Suicide: Theory and Practice in Elective Death. Amherst, NY: Humanity, 1999.

Lonny Shavelson
A Chosen Death: The Dying Confront Assisted Suicide. New York: Simon & Schuster, 1995.

Starhawk, M. Macha NightMare, and the Reclaiming Collective, eds.
The Pagan Book of Living and Dying: Practical Rituals, Prayers, Blessings, and Meditations on Crossing Over. New York: HarperCollins, 1998.

James L. Werth, ed.
Contemporary Perspectives on Rational Suicide. Philadelphia: Taylor & Francis, 1999.

Sue Woodman
Last Rights: The Struggle over the Right to Die. New York: Plenum, 1998.

Marjorie B. Zucker, ed.
The Right to Die Debate: A Documentary History. Westport, CT: Greenwood Press, 1999.

Periodicals

Barry A. Bostrom
"Physician-Assisted Suicide: Reflections on Oregon's First Case," *National Right to Life News,* March 15, 1999.

Norman L. Cantor
"Twenty-Five Years After Quinlan: A Review of the Jurisprudence of Death and Dying," *Journal of Law, Medicine & Ethics,* Summer 2001.

Kathryn Casey   "Let My Husband Die," *Ladies' Home Journal*, July 1999.

Gary Eisler   "Bonnie's Time: Even at the End, Life Is Precious," *Reader's Digest*, May 1998.

Ezekiel J. Emanuel   "Death's Door," *New Republic*, May 17, 1999.

Ezekiel J. Emanuel   "What Are the Potential Cost Savings from Legalizing
and Margaret P. Battin   Physician-Assisted Suicide?" *The New England Journal of Medicine*, July 16, 1998.

Ezekiel J. Emanuel,   "Attitudes and Desires Related to Euthanasia and
Diane L. Fairclough,   Physician-Assisted Suicide Among Terminally Ill Patients
and Linda L. Emanuel   and Their Caregivers," *JAMA*, November 15, 2000.

Franklin Foer and   "Death in Prime Time," *U.S. News & World Report*,
Sara Hammel   December 7, 1998.

Linda Ganzini,   "Attitudes of Patients with Amyotrophic Lateral Sclerosis
Wendy S. Johnston,   and Their Care Givers Toward Assisted Suicide," *New
Bentson H. McFarland,   England Journal of Medicine*, October 1, 1998.
Susan W. Tolle, and
Melinda A. Lee

Christine J. Gardner   "Severe Mercy in Oregon," *Christianity Today*, June 14, 1999.

Thomas Gates   "Euthanasia and Assisted Suicide: A Faith Perspective," *Friends Journal*, June 1998.

Erica Goode   "'Terminal Cancer Patient' Will to Live Is Found to Fluctuate," *New York Times*, September 4, 1999.

Jerome Groopman   "Separating Death from Agony: Ashcroft's Attack on Oregon's Law May Add Pain to Dying Everywhere," *New York Times*, November 9, 2001.

Herbert Hendlin,   "Physician-Assisted Suicide: Reflections on Oregon's First
Kathleen Foley,   Case," *Issues in Law & Medicine*, December 1, 1998.
and Margot White

Richard Horton   "Euthanasia and Assisted Suicide: What Does the Dutch Vote Mean?" *Lancet*, April 21, 2001.

Kevin Irvine   "Over My Dead Body," *POZ*, January 1998. Available from 349 West 12th St., New York, NY 10014-1721.

K.L. Braun Kayashima   "Examining the Variance in Support for Assisted Death Among Physicians, Patients, and the General Public," *Gerontologist*, October 15, 2001.

Paul R. McHugh   "Dying Made Easy," *Commentary*, February 1999.

Kathleen Dean Moore   "Do I Kill My Father?" *Commonweal*, June 19, 1998.

Russell D. Ogden   "Non-Physician Assisted Suicide: The Technological Imperative of the Deathing Counterculture," *Death Studies*, July 2001.

Betty Rollin   "Last Rights," *Ms.*, August/September 1999.

Joan R. Rose   "The Netherlands Finally Makes It Legal," *Medical Economics*, May 21, 2001.

Lewis P. Rowland — "Assisted Suicide and Alternatives in Amyotrophic Lateral Sclerosis," *New England Journal of Medicine*, October 1, 1998.

Maria J. Silveira, Albert DiPiero, Martha S. Gerrity, and Chris Feudtner — "Patients' Knowledge of Options at the End of Life: Ignorance in the Face of Death," *JAMA*, November 15, 2000.

Ruth Anne Van Loon — "Desire to Die in Terminally Ill People: A Framework for Assessment and Intervention," *Health and Social Work*, November 1999.

Adam Wolfson — "Killing Off the Dying?" *Public Interest*, Spring 1998.

Laura T. Worthen and Dale E. Yeatts — "Assisted Suicide: Factors Affecting Public Attitudes," *Omega—The Journal of Death and Dying (Farmindale)*, March 2001.

Index